May Oller W......
Wayne......

Workmen of God

Workmen of God

THE CURE OF SOULS

by

OSWALD CHAMBERS

GROSSET & DUNLAP

PUBLISHERS   NEW YORK

By arrangement with Dodd, Mead & Co.

Published in U. S. A., 1938,
By DODD, MEAD AND COMPANY, Inc.

7079

PRINTED IN THE U. S. A.

FOREWORD

ANOTHER book by Oswald Chambers! I wonder
if his eager readers think of him as a writer of
mature old age, giving the stored wisdom of a
long life in these searching, virile, helpful messages. If so, they are mistaken. The facts are that
his books are records of addresses and lectures
that he gave during a decade of wonderful public
and private ministry, both to students and congre-
gations who were privileged to listen to him between 1907 and 1917. His wife, with God-given
wisdom and energy, garnered this precious treas-
ure by taking verbatim reports in shorthand
throughout these busy years. Thus, when Oswald
Chambers suddenly and unexpectedly died in
Egypt in his early forties (during the Great War),
he left behind him a wealth of spiritual vitamins,
which have ever since been enriching us through
his books.

And now this latest book goes forth, at a time
when soul-sickness is more than ever rampant.
The messages are full of spiritual discernment and
diagnosis, and they were first given at Speke Hall,

Battersea, when Oswald Chambers was Principal of the Bible Training College at Clapham Common. Those of us who listened to him then, and worked with him, will never forget his forceful challenging statements, and we can never be thankful enough for the inspiration of his life and the blessing that resulted from his teaching.

He had a brilliant intellect, a highly trained disciplined mind and body, and an outstanding gift for teaching; but his great power lay in his consuming devotion to his Lord, in his entire reliance on the Holy Spirit, and in his absolute trust in the revelation of God through the Scriptures.

As these messages now go forth to a still wider circle, may they continually cause many to be wise in winning souls.

MARY R. HOOKER.

RIDGELANDS COLLEGE,
WIMBLEDON.
April, 1937.

CONTENTS

Chapter I

HOW TO WORK FOR THE CURE OF SOULS

"And David said, There is none like that; give it me." 1 Samuel xxi. 9.

THE setting is known to us all. David is talking about Goliath's sword, and he asks for it, "give it me." We read the passage in Deuteronomy where Moses said to the children of Israel, "the cause that is too hard for you, bring it unto me, and I will hear it" (Deuteronomy i. 17). I want to take these two Old Testament mighty men of God as types of what the worker for God must be like to work for the cure of souls.

With regard to the sword that there is none like it, if you will turn to Hebrews iv. 12, you will see how I want to take Goliath's sword and spiritualize it in the hands of a worker for God among the children of men: "For the word of God is living, and active, and sharper than any two-edged sword, and piercing even to the dividing of soul and spirit, of both joints and marrow, and quick to

1

discern the thoughts and intents of the heart."
Now it is quite obvious that if you are not David
and are trying to use Goliath's sword, you will do
far more harm to yourself than damage to the
enemy. You must be in the direct line of succes-
sion to David. David and Moses were mighty
giants, but we have to be of the same family connection. What is the same family connection in
this dispensation? Why, those who are born again
of the Spirit of God, and those who are so identi-
fied with the Lord Jesus that they have entered
into the experience of entire sanctification. When
they use the word of God they do not damage
themselves, nor hurt other souls; but they do great
damage to the kingdom of the devil and bring
benefit to the souls of men.

Before we take up the question of the kind of
souls we shall have to deal with, we must deal with
the worker. Now there are big difficulties in the
way. The first difficulty is that we are not dealing
with men's bodies. If we were, we could be taught
in special schools and colleges, trained and de-
veloped in such a way that we should know fairly
well how to apply principles to the various ailments of people, because physical ailments have a
wonderful likeness to each other. This has led
many Christian workers astray; they think that

because men's bodies and bodily ailments are alike, and because one cure, carefully and judiciously prescribed by a physician who diagnosed the case aright was successful and can be applied to other cases with similar results, that men's souls can be treated in the same way. But you cannot deal with the human soul and with the ailments and difficulties of the human soul according to any principle whatever. I think that any of you who have worked for God know this, that immediately you get into the way of using certain verses of Scripture and applying them to those who are seeking new birth, and certain other verses to those seeking sanctification, you will find suddenly that God's Spirit will depart from you and He will not use those verses in your hands any more. The reason is this, that immediately we get wedded to a short-cut in dealing with souls, God leaves us alone.

The first thing I want to lay down for the worker (I am talking about one who really is born again of the Spirit of God and has been entirely sanctified) is that he or she must rely on the Holy Spirit to direct them as to what to say in the case of every soul that comes. Do not rely on your memory, do not remember how you dealt with cases in the past, but recognize and rely on the

Holy Spirit that He will bring to your remembrance the particular verse for you to apply at this time. You will find over and over again that God will bring confusion to your methods and will make you apply a text to sanctification which you in your system have said can only be applied to new birth; and He will make you apply a text which you have said can only apply to sanctification to something else, and you will make incessant blunders in work for God if you are not careful and watchful and heedful of the guidance of the Holy Spirit and of His bringing the word of God to your remembrance. Remember, then, that the worker who is rightly related to God must ever rely on the Holy Spirit for guidance in each individual case.

Then I want to apply Moses' statement: "The cause that is too hard for you, bring it unto me." Do you know how to bring your cases to God? We all know how to bring them to one another and how to talk to Christian workers about dealing with souls, but just as there are quack doctors in the medical profession, so there is the same thing in the spiritual domain. Beware of anything that does not fling you straight back in reliance on the Holy Spirit as the most practical factor you know in bringing to your remembrance the word

4

of God and how to apply it.

Then another thing—the worker must live among the facts he has to deal with. Regarding the training of workers, take the highest class we know of, ministers. One of the greatest difficulties in most of our colleges for training ministers, who are supposed to work for the cure of souls, is that they are never taught how to deal with souls. There is hardly a college anywhere for training ministers where the question of dealing with souls is ever mentioned. Ministers will bear me out in this, that everything they have learned they have had to learn out of their own experience. They are trained in everything but how to deal with the facts they have to deal with.

There are two kinds of facts the worker must be amongst—he must go to school among human souls. I mean we must keep ourselves in touch, not with theories, but with people, and never get out of touch with human beings, if we are going to use the word of God skilfully amongst them, and if the Holy Spirit is to apply the word of God through us as workmen needing not to be ashamed. Live among your human facts, and you will find how continually God stirs up your nest. If you are a worker, He will constantly surround you with different kinds of people, with different difficulties, and He will constantly put you to school amongst those facts. He will keep you in contact with human stuff, and human stuff is very sordid; in fact, human stuff is made of just the same stuff as you and I are made of; do not shut yourself away from it. Beware of the tendency to live a life apart and shut away. Get amongst men. Jesus prayed, "I pray not that Thou shouldest take them out of the world, but that Thou shouldest keep them from the evil."

Then there is another series of facts, viz., Bible facts. We have to go to school among human souls, and we have to educate ourselves in Bible facts. A remarkable thing about this Book of God (and I hope, by God's grace, to point this out) is that for every type of human being we come across there is a distinct, clear line laid down here as to the way to apply God's truth to it. The stupid soul, the stubborn soul, the soul that is mentally diseased, the soul that is convicted of sin, the soul with the twisted mind, the sensual soul—every one of the facts that you meet in your daily walk and business has its counterpart here, and God has a word and a revelation fact with regard to every life you come across.

Let me emphasize these three things again: First, the Christian worker who is right with God must rely every moment on the Holy Spirit when dealing with another soul. Second, the worker must live among human facts, men and women, not theories. Do not let us tell ourselves what men and women are like, let us find out what they are like. One of the greatest mistakes in the world is to tell yourself what a man is like; you do not know what he is like. The only One Who can teach you how to deal with the various specimens around you is the Holy Spirit. The third thing is, ransack this old Book from cover to cover in the most practical way you know—by using a concordance, by re-writing the Psalms, or by any other immediate practical method.

I know it is customary to ridicule certain ways in which some people say God guides them, but I am very chary about ridiculing any methods. For example, it is easy to ridicule this kind of method: 'Lord, direct me to a word, I am just going to shut my eyes and open the Book and put my finger on a passage.' I say it is easy to ridicule it, yet it is absurd to say that God has not led people in that way; He has. Why I mention these facts is to knock certain theories to pieces. You cannot tie God down to a particular line. You will find that God does use the most extraordinary methods people adopt; only do not take anyone else's way,

7

get to know how God deals with you, and how He deals with others through you in the most practical way.

Keep these three things in mind—reliance on the Holy Spirit of God, keeping in contact with people and, above all, keeping in contact with the revelation facts in God's Book; live amongst them, and ask God how to apply them.

Another thing I want to mention—never believe what people tell you about themselves. There is only one person in a thousand who can actually tell you his or her symptoms; and beware of the people who can tell you where they are spiritually. I mean by that, never be guided by what people tell you; rely on the Spirit of God all the time you are probing them.

Let me read you this in regard to medical treatment,—

"Recent evidence in the law courts has pointed to a fact which the medical profession holds of great value— the necessity, not only of personal and private interview with a patient, but of the penetrative ability to get at the real facts and symptoms. In other words, successful diagnosis depends on the doctor's acumen in cross-examination.

'Cross-examination of a patient is almost always necessary,' says an eminent medical man. 'They will give me causes, or rather what they think are causes, instead

8

of symptoms. The rich patient is more troublesome in this respect than the poor, for he has had leisure in which to evolve a sort of scheme of his illness, based on "popular" medical knowledge.

'Patients always colour facts, speaking absolutely instead of relatively. They never tell the truth about the amount of sleep they have had or as to appetite. They frequently say they have had nothing to eat. Casually you find there were two eggs at least for breakfast. A minute or two later they remember stewed steak for dinner.

'Perhaps the greatest need for cross-examination is that it gives an extended opportunity to the medical man to examine the patient objectively. The most important symptoms are generally those the patient never notices.' "

If that is true in the medical profession which deals with men's bodies, it is a thousandfold more true about spiritual symptoms when it comes to dealing with a man's soul. Do beware, then, of paying too much attention to the talk of the one that is in trouble, keep your own heart and mind alert on what God is saying to you; get to the place where you will know when the Holy Spirit brings the word of God to your remembrance for that one.

Now there is a wrong use of God's word and a right one. The wrong use is this sort of thing—someone comes to you, and you cast about in your mind what sort of man he is, then hurl a text at him like a projectile, either in prayer or in talking as you deal with him. That is a use of the word of God that kills your own soul and the souls of the people you deal with. The Spirit of God is not in that. Jesus said, "The words I speak unto you, they are spirit, and they are life." "Who also hath made us able ministers of the new testament; not of the letter, but of the spirit: for the letter killeth, but the spirit giveth life." Do remember to keep your soul in unsullied touch with the directions of the Spirit.

Another thing that is very puzzling is this. Probably all of you have had experiences as I have on this line: you listen to clear Bible teaching, unmistakably clear, almost taking people by the hand and leading them straight into the Kingdom of God, but they never come. Another time a man gets up and twists everything, and to your astonishment people are born again. That frequently happened in Water Street Mission in New York, a man who had been wonderfully saved would get up and tell what he had been and what he was now, then others would do the same, and the Spirit of God got hold of the people before you knew where you were, out they came to the altar, and these rough men knelt down and prayed with them and they 'struck something,' as they say out there, and something 'struck them,' and they were wonderfully born again.

Now these are facts we have to look at. You cannot put God down to a prescribed method. These souls were real, living, good specimens of what God had done, and the Spirit of God worked through them. I mention that because it confuses a great amount of our reasoning in Christian work; over and over again you will find that some poor, ignorant servant, or artisan, who seems scarcely to know how to put anything together, is used of God mightily in the salvation of souls, and others who have a clear understanding of the whole thing and put the way of salvation ever so clearly, yet nothing happens. So all we can get at is the main methods laid down in God's Book about the worker. Let us ask ourselves, 'Do I experimentally know what the salvation of God is? Do I know what entire sanctification means in my own experience?' The worker for God must be in a healthy, vigorous, spiritual condition himself.

I want to say one word of criticism about the choosing of Sunday-school teachers. The way Sunday-school teachers are chosen is that immediately a person gets introduced into the Kingdom of God, they are given a Sunday-school class to teach. When you come to God's way, you will find

11

something very different; immediately a soul gets introduced into the Kingdom of God, it has got to do something, but it is something along the line of the new life it has received, obedience and walking in the light, until it is consolidated in the ways of God. Why is this necessary? Because dealing with souls is tenfold more dangerous than dealing with bodies. Unless you are in a healthy, vigorous condition with God, you will catch the disease of the soul you are dealing with instead of helping to cure it. Unless you are out amongst the tremendous facts of God's revelation in the Bible, unless you know how to take breezy walks through that Book, unless you know how to walk up and down that country and take in the air of God's hills and get thoroughly robust and continually change your walk amongst those facts, you are sure to catch the diseases of the souls you are dealing with. So remember, it is absolutely necessary to be like the cedars of Lebanon. Do you know the characteristic of a Lebanon tree? The cedars of Lebanon have such extraordinary power of life that instead of nourishing parasites it kills them, the life within is so strong and so robust that instead of feeding the parasites it chokes them off. God grant that we may be so filled with His life, may flourish as the cedars of Lebanon, so that He

12

can trust us down in all the dark, difficult places amongst the souls of our brother men and be able to pour His tremendous health and power through us.

How sad it is to see men and women who did begin to work for God, and whose work God honoured, slowly fall off. Why? They have caught the disease of death amongst the people they have been dealing with. In the medical profession, particularly doctors who deal with the insane, have continually to be changed, continually shifted. Why? Because they take the diseases and troubles they live amongst, and you will find that God the Holy Ghost has an amazing power of shifting His workers. Some wonder why God keeps shifting them, why He shifts their circumstances; the reason is not only to keep them in touch with the great sphere of work, but to keep their souls alive.

Do remember, then, that it is necessary for the worker to be healthy, and beware of this mistake, that by working for God amongst men, you develop your own Christian life; you do not unless your Christian life is there first. It is so obvious that it needs to be said over again—you cannot develop your own Christian life unless it is there. The advice given that if you work for God you develop your own life often means that if you work for God you get right yourself; you do not, you have to be right with God first.

The next time you deal with a soul at the penitent form, remember it is one thing to tell him to receive the Spirit of God, to recognize and rely on Him, but quite another thing for you to do the same thing. Unless you recognize the Spirit of God, and rely on Him, and expect Him to bring to your remembrance some word that is going to apply in that case, you will be of very little use as an expert soul-curer and for putting people in the way to get right with God.

Then do live among human facts! Thank God He has given the majority of us the surroundings of real, definite, sordid human beings; there is no pretence about them, the people we live among and come in contact with are not theories, they are facts. That is the kind of thing God wants us to keep among.

Then third, see that you get into this Book. I feel more than hungry to see men and women roused up to get hold of this Book and live among its facts, then the Spirit of God will bring to your remembrance how to apply the truth in each case.

Chapter II

THE WORKER AMONG THE ABNORMAL

"For the Son of man is come to seek and to save that which was lost." Luke xix. 10.

ABNORMAL means not normal or according to rule, not upright, not good. God's Book says that the whole of the human race is abnormal.

In our first talk we dealt with the Christian worker, and we found that first of all he must have a definite experience in his own life of the marvellous salvation of God. Then that he must learn how to recognize and rely on the Spirit of God in dealing with souls; he must live in the facts of the Bible, and keep in touch with the facts of human life. Now we deal with some of the facts of human life as God's Book reveals them.

I want to notice a very important distinction, viz., that the 'lost' from the Bible standpoint are not doomed. The lost, Jesus Christ is seeking for; the doomed are those who rebel against the seeking Saviour. To Jesus Christ, all men are lost, and the worker who is going to work for the cure of souls must have the same outlook. We have to bear this in mind because workers to-day are not taking the standpoint of the Lord Jesus Christ.

In Luke xix. we find a specimen of a lost man. "The Son of man is come to seek and to save that which was lost." Notice the setting of this statement. Zacchæus was a chief publican and as such he would be possessed of many ill-gotten gains; he was a man of wealth and position, a dishonourable man, but perfectly content with his dishonour. Zacchæus was not troubled in the tiniest degree, his whole nature towards God was frozen, no sign of life about him. In the far North the thermometer freezes and can record nothing, and it remains frozen until the temperature alters; immediately the temperature alters, then the thermometer registers. This man Zacchæus was frozen towards God, his conscience did not bother him, he was 'lost,' quite contented, quite happy, and quite curious. When Jesus Christ came his way, the man's nature unfroze, something began to work at once.

The first thing the worker has to learn is how to bring the Lord Jesus Christ in contact with frozen souls, those who are dead towards God, whose consciences are not the slightest bit disturbed. How is the worker to bring the Lord Jesus Christ

16

across the life that is dead in trespasses and sins and does not know it? By the Holy Spirit and personal experience alone. By personal experience I mean what we have already insisted on: I must know personally what God has done in my soul through Jesus Christ; and I must have learned how to rely on the Holy Spirit, because the Holy Spirit makes Jesus Christ present to all kinds and conditions of men. The majority of people when they come across a nature like Zacchæus will say he is simply selfish, sordid and indifferent; he is not convicted of sin, it is no use to try and deal with him. That is the attitude we all maintain to the 'Zacchæus' type of man until we learn how to bring Jesus Christ close to him. Whenever Jesus Christ came across men in His day, they knew where they were, and they either rebelled or followed Him. They either went away exceeding sorrowful, or they turned with their whole nature towards Him.

The next thing we have to learn by contact with Jesus Christ is this, that if the whole human race —everybody, good, bad and indifferent—is lost, we must have the boundless confidence of Jesus Christ Himself about us, that is, we must know that He can save anybody and everybody. There is a great deal of importance to be attached to this point. Just reflect in your mind and think of some lives you know that are frozen; there is no conviction of sin; they are dishonourable, and they know it; they are abnormal, off the main track altogether, but they are not a bit troubled about it; talk to them about their wrong-doing and they are totally indifferent to you. You have to learn how to introduce the atmosphere of the Lord Jesus Christ around those souls. As soon as you do, something happens. Look what happened to Zacchæus—"And Zacchæus stood, and said unto the Lord, Behold, Lord, the half of my goods I give to the poor; and if I have wrongfully exacted aught of any man, I restore him fourfold." Who had been talking to him about his doings? Not a soul. Jesus had never said a word about his evil doings. What awakened him? What suddenly made him know where he was? The presence of Jesus!

Wherever a worker for God goes, the same thing will happen if the Spirit of God is getting His way through that man or woman. If you are right with God in personal experience, saved and sanctified (to use our own technical words), and the Spirit of God is getting His way with you, other people will get to know where they are wrong, and until they learn the reason they will say you are criticizing them; but you are perfectly conscious that you have never criticized them. What has happened? This very thing, the Holy Spirit's presence through you, has brought the atmosphere that Jesus Christ's presence always brought, and has thawed the ice around their mind and their conscience and they are beginning to be convicted.

Let me insist that the worker must know how to bring every kind and condition of man into contact with Jesus Christ, and the only way that can be done is by reliance on the Holy Spirit and by personal experience. If you are trying to work for God and have no definite experience of your own and do not know how to rely on the Holy Spirit, God grant that you may come to the place where you do know, then wherever you go the atmosphere produced will thaw things around men's consciences and hearts.

Men's minds will always assent that Jesus Christ is right,—why? Because Jesus Christ is Incarnate Reason. There is something in Jesus Christ that appeals to every man, no matter what condition he is in. If once Jesus Christ is brought into contact with a man, let that man seem to us dead and indifferent, destitute of anything like goodness—let him come in contact with Jesus Christ by the

Holy Spirit, and you will instantly see that he can grasp something about Him in a way we cannot understand unless we know the Holy Spirit.

Jesus Christ always appeals to men's consciences, —why? Because He is Incarnate Righteousness. So many people try to explain things about Jesus Christ, but no worker need ever try to do that. You cannot explain things about Jesus Christ, rely on the Holy Spirit and He will explain Jesus to the soul. Let me recommend you to have this boundless confidence in Jesus Christ's power as you go into work for God! If you do not believe practically in your heart that the Lord Jesus Christ can alter and save the man you are talking to, you limit Jesus Christ in that life. You may say, 'Oh, yes, Jesus Christ can save you; He can alter the whole thing and can put His new life within you and make you a new man'; but if *you* do not believe He can do it, you limit God's power in that life, and God holds you responsible. So the first thing the worker must do is to keep his heart always believing in Jesus.

Are you in constant contact with frozen natures in your own family, in your business, in your friendships? You have talked with them, prayed with them, you have done everything you know how, but there is not the slightest sign of conviction of sin, no trouble of conscience or heart. They are not 'out-and-out' sinners, but you know that they are 'in-and-in' sinners; you know they are wrong and twisted and have things that are not clean, but you cannot make them realize it; they always get away, frozen and untouched. Then bring your own soul face to face with Jesus Christ: 'Lord, do *I* believe that Thou canst thaw that man's nature, that woman's nature, until the Holy Spirit has a chance of saving him or her?' That is the first difficulty to be overcome—what state of faith in Jesus Christ have I? Then next ask yourself, 'Do I believe that the Lord Jesus Christ can take that selfish, sensual, twisted, self-satisfied nature that is all wrong and out of order—do I believe that He can make it perfect in the sight of God?' Oh, do let us get back to this tremendous confidence in the Lord Jesus Christ's power! back to reliance on the Holy Spirit, and to remembering that Jesus came to seek the lost.

In the fifteenth chapter of St. Luke's Gospel, our Lord speaks about the joy of finding lost things, and to me there is always this appeal: the Lord wants my eyes to look through; is He looking through them? The Lord wants my brain to think through; is He thinking through it? The Lord wants my hands to work with; is He working with them? The Lord wants my body to live and walk in for one purpose—to go after the lost from His standpoint; am I letting Him walk and live in me?

The worker must see that Jesus Christ has His right of way in him in each particular. Oh, the number of men and women to-day who are working on the line of self-realization; seeking the training of the mind and of the body—for what purpose? To help them realize themselves! Jesus Christ wants this body so that He can work through it to find those who are out of the way. Do remember that it is the most practical thing on this earth to be a worker for the cure of souls. You have to rely on the Holy Spirit and to live among human facts and Bible facts. Have you, Christian worker, accepted the verdict of Jesus Christ regarding the human race, viz., that they are all lost, and have you got boundless confidence in Jesus Christ, are you perfectly certain that if a soul can only get in contact with Jesus, He can save him absolutely?

I want to give one word of warning to workers for God, especially Sunday-school teachers and preachers of the Gospel—beware of the snare of putting anything first in your mind but Jesus Christ. If you put the needs of your people first, there is something between you and the power of God. Face Jesus Christ steadily, and allow nothing, no work and no person, to come between you and Him. For what purpose? That the Holy Spirit may flow through you in your preaching to the needs of the people around. You will find that people will always distinguish between that kind of message and the message that is spoken out of sympathy with them. There is only one Being Who understands us all and that is the Holy Spirit, and He understands the Lord Jesus Christ too, and if you keep the avenues of your soul open to Him and get your messages from Him and see that you allow nothing to obscure Him, you will find He will locate the people. For every new message you give, God will give you human beings who have been convicted by it, and you will have to deal with them, whether you like it or not; and you will have not only to deal with them, but you will have to take them on your heart before God. God will make you work for the cure of the souls He has wounded by your message. If the wounding has come along His line, the line of the faithful proclamation of His message, He will let you see Him healing that soul through you as a worker, as you rely on the Holy Spirit. God grant that as we go forth to our varied work we may be filled with the Spirit, and then patiently do the drudgery!

I want to say one other thing that will connect this talk with the next one—the Spirit of God will not work for the cure of some souls without you, and God is going to hold to the account of some of us the souls that have gone un-cured, un-healed, un-touched by Jesus Christ because we have refused to keep our souls open towards Him, and when the sensual, selfish, wrong lives came around we were not ready to present the Lord Jesus Christ to them by the power of the Holy Spirit. Workers for God, let us believe with all our heart these Divine revelations, and never despair of any soul under heaven. If you have a chronic case—I mean by that, someone who is always coming out at every altar call but never getting anywhere, thank God for it. I have found this out, that as far as I am concerned, God uses those chronic seekers as an education to me. It is a tremendous temptation to put them on one side and say, 'It is no use dealing with such people.' It is! If they keep chronic long enough they will educate you so sufficiently that the Lord will be able to manifest His patience through you as He never could otherwise, and all of a sudden those souls will come into the light.

Chapter III

THE WORKER AMONG THE HARDY ANNUALS

"For there are no bands in their death: but their strength is firm." Psalm lxxiii. 4.

By 'hardy annuals' I mean the healthy-minded sinners. We pointed out before that from Jesus Christ's point of view all men are lost, but we have so narrowed and so specialized the term 'lost' that we have missed its evangelical meaning; we have made it mean that only the people who are down and out in sin are lost.

In the seventeenth chapters of Acts we see Paul the Pharisee, and the sanctified Apostle of God, face to face with healthy-minded, vigorous pagans. Jesus Christ came in contact with such people over and over again, and you will find that you have to come in contact with them too. They are once-born people, and perfectly content with being once-born. They are usually upright, quite sufficient for themselves morally, very bright and happy, and you seem to feel they have not the slightest need of the Lord Jesus Christ in their lives. That class formed a great setting all round our Lord's life. In the days of His flesh our Lord worked almost exclusively amongst Jews, but every now and again a Gentile burst through into the inner circle, and Jesus always dealt with him in a totally different manner. Whenever our Lord dealt with a religious Jew there was a serious solemnity about Him, and a serious solemnity about the Jew; but immediately our Lord came in contact with a Greek, He seemed to read the sharp wit of the Greek straightaway and dealt with him accordingly.

In the fifteenth chapter of St. Matthew we read that our Lord departed into the coasts of Tyre and Sidon, the reason being that He wanted to be alone; He had had too much publicity and was trying to get His disciples away. Then a Syrophœnician woman burst through with a request to which Jesus pays no attention, the reason being quite obvious—He wanted to be quiet, and He knew perfectly well that this woman would blaze abroad more than ever what He could do. But her faith was strong, she knew that if she could get hold of the Lord Jesus He would heal her daughter. Watch how our Lord deals with her; He gives her a proverb and she gives Him back a proverb:

"It is not meet to take the children's bread and cast it to the dogs." "Yea, Lord: for even the dogs eat of the crumbs which fall from their masters' table." Her type of mind was foreign to the religious Jews, but Jesus understood her at once, and He praised her for her faith. "O woman, great is thy faith: be it done unto thee even as thou wilt."

The healthy-minded tendency is very strong to-day. It is the explanation of Unitarianism in its shallower aspect; the explanation of the New Thought movement and the Mind Cure movement, of Christian Science; it is the explanation of how people can be quite happy, quite moral, quite upright, without having anything to do with the Lord Jesus Christ. Our Lord describes these people in terms of the once-born, as 'lost.' The problem for us as workers is, how are we to get these irreligious people who are quite happy and healthy-minded, to the place where they want Jesus?

The Syrophœnician woman came to our Lord at the end of a busy spell, and you will find that these healthy-minded folks will often come across you when you are fagged out and will ask you all kinds of questions. They did of the Apostle Paul— "What would this babbler say? . . . He seemeth to be a setter forth of strange gods: because he preached Jesus and the resurrection." In writing to the Corinthians, Paul says, "We preach Christ crucified . . . unto the Greeks foolishness."

Every worker for God has surely come across the type of man that makes him feel foolish; the external life, and internal life as far as you know, is quite sterling and upright, and he puts questions to you that bring you to a complete standstill, you cannot answer them, and he succeeds in making you feel amazingly foolish. For instance, you preach that Jesus Christ lived and died and rose again to save men from their sins and to put them right with God; these people have no sin that they are conscious of, you cannot point to a spot in their whole life, they are healthy-minded and happy, but absolutely pagan, and they say, 'What was the use of Jesus Christ dying for me? I am all right; I do exactly what I ought to do. I am not a blackguard, I am not a thief, I am not a sinner. Why ever should Jesus Christ die for me?' Unless you are used to it, that line of thing produces a sense of unutterable foolishness in you. How are we to bring the Gospel of Jesus Christ, and our Lord Himself, before a man or woman of that sort?

I want us to look at three types of pagans—Gallio, Herod and Pilate. Gallio was an ordinary pagan, upright and just, and when the Apostle Paul was brought before him he did not care anything about him. "And Gallio cared for none of those things." He said in effect, 'I have nothing whatever to do with your religious quarrels, I am not here to decide questions of your law for you.' The opponents of Christianity are not weak, they are opponents who are able to ignore us; so the first thing to do is to examine and see what kind of Gospel we are preaching. If you are only preaching before this kind of pagan, upright, righteous and just, but without a spark of religion in him, that Jesus Christ can save sinners, that is not the Jesus Christ he needs. You have to preach the Lord Jesus Christ revealed in God's Word.

The first thing I want to impress on our hearts and minds as workers is this—we must not preach one phase of Christ's work. Jesus said, "I, if I be lifted up from the earth, will draw all men unto Myself." Have I a pet doctrine I am lifting up? If I have, then these healthy-minded folk will simply heap ridicule on me; but immediately I preach Christ, something happens—the Spirit of God begins to work where I cannot. The first point for us to remember then, is that we must preach Christ, not a pet theory of our own, no matter how right and true it is, no matter how important a doctrine or how really the outcome of our Lord's work; that is not what we have to present, we have to present Jesus Christ. "And Philip . . . preached unto him Jesus." (Acts viii. 35.)

Paul was able to stand the ridicule, the cultured ridicule, of the Athenian philosophers because he knew Jesus Christ, he knew Him as the greatest, grandest and most worthy Being that was ever on this earth. See that you present the Lord Jesus Christ Himself to your ordinary pagan. The Spirit of God will guide you as you rely on Him to the presentation that is required for each one. Some people present Jesus Christ in packets, they have one packet of verses marked 'Salvation,' another marked 'Sanctification,' another marked 'The Baptism with the Holy Ghost.' The reason they do this is easy to understand—these particular verses have been used mightily in their experience in saving souls, but as we pointed out at the first, immediately we begin to depend on our special prescription the Spirit of God will depart from us. In every case we have to deal with, whether it be the case of a man with a frozen conscience, or a healthy-minded pagan, we have to learn how to rely on the Holy Spirit straightaway—'Lord, this man is healthy, his sense of justice clear, his record clean, but he cares for none of these things; I

30

cannot deal with him.' We have to present Jesus Christ in all His power, and rely on the Holy Spirit to deal with him.

There is another type of pagan and he is represented by Herod. Herod is a rare type of pagan, he is obscene; he was bad, unmentionably bad, and you will find that when he saw Jesus Christ face to face he was not the slightest bit troubled. Why? He had heard the voice of God before through John the Baptist, and he had ordered that voice to be silent. Herod is the presentation of the awful possibility of a fixed character, absolutely fixed in immorality. Jesus Christ did not awaken one tremor of conscience in him, he had signed his own death-warrant. When the voice of God came to him in repeated warnings through John the Baptist about the thing that was wrong in his life, he would not listen, he persisted in his badness until he killed all his affinity for God, and when Jesus Christ stood before him he was not an atom troubled. Did you ever notice what is recorded? "Now when Herod saw Jesus, he was exceeding glad"—why? For the same reason that people go to a picture show, they want to see things. We read that Herod questioned Jesus in many words; "but He answered him nothing." "There is a sin unto death"—there is a final apos-

tasy from God, there is a sealed doom on an im-
mortal soul while it lives, where God Almighty
cannot awaken one echo of response—"I do not say
that he shall pray for it," says John. (1 John v. 16,
R.V.)

If you have never faced the question yourself,
face it now—you are not as bothered now as you
once were, if you are bothered at all, about Jesus
Christ's line of things, and you are to blame; there
will come a time when you will not be bothered
even as much as you are now. Once Herod heard
John the Baptist gladly. (Mark vi. 20.) If God
has ever pointed out to you in the past the one
thing that is wrong in your life, you are to blame
if you did not listen. A time will come when all
the tremendous presentation of the truth of God
will become a farce. God forbid that any worker
should ever stand face to face with a son of perdition, with a man or woman who has apostatized
from God. There is such a thing as fixity of character, and when one's prayers go out for such an
one they are arrested by God, not by the devil,
and frozen before they get out of the lips. This is
a truth, an awful and terrible truth, but one that
people will not listen to.

Another type of pagan is Pilate. Pilate represents the type of pagan who always seeks his own

interests; that type is known to us all to-day. People belong to certain churches because it is better for their business; or they shift their membership to other churches because it is more convenient for business. A once-born man who acts from this point of view is an opportunist. 'If it is Jesus Christ's Gospel that is in the ascendancy, then I will use it to serve my own ends.' You have to bring that man face to face with Christ, not with your experience, but with Jesus Christ Himself.

Gallio is a type of the ordinary pagan, healthy-minded, vigorous, strong and happy. Is it right to be healthy-minded? Of course it is. Is it right to be happy? Of course it is. That is why the new phases of thought we have alluded to are spreading and putting down Christianity. If you can teach a man how to ignore sin, you have him. If you can tell him how to ignore pain successfully and disease and trouble, he will listen to you. If you can tell him how to ignore the possibility of judgment coming on him for wrong-doing, he will listen to you. If you can show a man how he can be delivered from the torture of sin, delivered from a pain-stricken body, loosened from a bad past, then you have him. Mark you, every one of these points is right; the prince of this world delivers on that line, and so does the Lord Jesus

33

Christ. Watch Jesus Christ's life—the people would take all His blessings, but they would not get rightly related to Him; and our difficulty is in presenting men with Jesus Christ apart from what He can do. How does Jesus Christ teach a man to forget sin? By forgiving him. How does a pagan teach a man to forget sin? 'Ignore it, think no more about it, realize yourself!' Can it be done? Of course it can be done. If you will just sin long enough, you will forget how sinful you have been, and is it likely that a man who has forgotten how wrong he has been is going to be willing to face Jesus Christ, who, as soon as He sees him, will flash through him his past wrong? The first thing Jesus Christ does is to open a man's eyes wide to the wrong and then deliver him from it. If anyone here is getting to the place of forgetting sin by ignoring it, the place of healthy-mindedness and happiness without facing the past wrong, that is the characteristic of the pagan; but Jesus will open our eyes wide to see the wrong and will deliver us from it by putting us on another platform.

The Syrophœnician woman wanted the Lord Jesus Christ. She did not care one iota about the disciples, what she wanted was the Lord Jesus Christ. Again we read that certain Greeks came to the disciples saying, "Sir, we would see Jesus."

What did those disciples do? They went and told Jesus. Christian worker, when anyone belonging to the healthy pagan type comes to your meeting, whose presence there means "We would see Jesus," what do you do? Try and persuade him? You never will. Remember what Philip and Andrew did—they went and told Jesus. Whenever you get the request, either by presence or by word: "We would see Jesus," don't begin with 'firstly, secondly and thirdly,' go to Jesus and say, 'Lord, these people want to see Thee.'

Again we come back to our first points—rely on the Holy Ghost as the most practical Being you ever knew, and live among the facts of God's Word and among human facts, and people will recognize Jesus Christ through you. God grant that every worker may ever remember that the only One Who can touch 'the hardy annuals' whom no truth seems to upset, who carry bright, cheerful faces, and no adversity turns them aside, is the Lord Jesus Christ Himself. People say that it is so hard to bring Jesus Christ and present Him before the lives of men to-day. Of course it is, it is so hard that it is impossible except by the power of the indwelling Holy Ghost. A crisis comes in every man's life. The 107th Psalm is a record of people who would not come to God until they were at their wits' end. When they were at their wits' end, then they cried to God and He heard them.

If you go and tell men it is better to be good than bad, they will say, 'Yes, that is so, but how are you going to make bad men good?' That is the problem. Unless your religion will go to the lowest and the worst and the most desperate case you know of, your religion is of no use. There are a great many forms of belief which cannot begin to touch the worst of mankind, they can only deal with cultured minds and hearts. Jesus Christ's religion goes down to the lowest of the low as well as up to the highest of the high, and to all in between. The marvel of Jesus Christ is that He takes facts as they are. He Himself is the answer to every problem of heart and mind and life. The next time you come across a 'hardy annual,' see that you lay hold of God for that one until Jesus Christ is presented by the power of the Holy Ghost, and then you will see the altered face, the altered attitude, and the altered life.

Chapter IV

THE WORKER AMONG BACKSLIDERS

"And on some have mercy with fear; hating even the garment spotted by the flesh." Jude 23 (R.V.).

THE best example of a backslider in the New Testament (the word 'backslider' is never used in the New Testament, it is an Old Testament word) is in 2 Timothy iv. 10. "For Demas forsook me, having loved this present world"—he has gone back to where he prefers. Couple with that Jeremiah ii. 13, and you will have a good indication of what a backslider is: "For My people have committed two evils; they have forsaken Me the fountain of living waters, and hewed them out cisterns, broken cisterns, that can hold no water." Backsliding is twofold, and the term can only be applied to people in this condition. We use the word very loosely, we apply it to people who are degenerating, to people who have committed sin; but a backslider is neither one nor the other, a backslider is worse than both. He is worse than a person who is degenerating, and worse than a person who has committed sin; he has forsaken God and taken up with something else.

It is customary to talk of Peter as being a back-slider when he denied his Lord; what happened to Peter was that he got a revelation of what he was capable of, viz., of denying his Lord with oaths and curses. What were the conditions that led to Peter's fall? He had followed Jesus out of genu-ine devotion, and in true loyalty of heart to Jesus he had pictured a great many things that might happen, but never in his wildest moment did he imagine that Jesus Christ was tamely going to give Himself up to the powers of the world, and when Peter saw Jesus Christ quietly give Himself right over to the rabble and let them take Him, all Peter's thoughts were turned into con-fusion, his heart was in despair, and in that condition, he "followed afar off." Then when he was tormented by stinging questions, he suddenly found in himself this awful condition he was to-tally ignorant of, a condition that made him deny with oaths and curses that he ever knew Jesus. Re-member, Peter belonged to a dispensation we can-not begin to imagine, a dispensation before Jesus Christ died and rose again; but if we do not live in the dispensation Peter lived in, we can understand the people he represents. Peter was loyal-hearted and devoted to Jesus, but grossly ignorant of what he was capable of—quite loyal, but quite ignorant, and in the trying crisis suddenly to his amazement he finds that he is capable of evil that horrifies him.

The way God deals with a backslider, and teaches us to deal with a backslider, is clear enough for us to talk about it now.

Let us first of all examine for ourselves and find out whether in using the word 'backslider' we are applying it to the right condition of a man. The backslidden condition is twofold: it is forsaking God and taking up with something else; it is not the condition of a man awakening to the presence of the disposition of sin in himself. A backslider is a man who does know what God's grace is, who does know what sin is, and who does know what deliverance is, but who has deliberately forsaken God and gone back because he loved something else better.

The question is often asked, 'Can a Christian sin?' He certainly can, but the sin must be confessed immediately and forgiven, for if a Christian allows an act of sin to go on it will lead him steadily on until he will pervert all the ways of God and hew out a way for himself.

The statement is frequently made that in dealing with a backslider, the worker has to bring him to being born again of the Spirit. A backslider has not to be born again, he is in a much worse condition than a man not born again: he has to have his backslidings healed and be restored. The statements in the Bible about backsliding are very solemn. Backsliding is the most awful crime spiritually; it is forsaking God and hewing out for one's self "broken cisterns, that can hold no water." With a backslider it is not the question of a soul needing to be born again, but a much harder case than a man who has never been born again. Do not get confused because when you have to face backsliders you find you cannot deal with them as you deal with any ordinary sinner. Their hearts are frozen, they are not convicted of sin, they are absolutely dull and dead towards all God wants. They will tell you quite mechanically, 'Oh yes, I once knew God, I did experience this and that, but I deliberately stepped aside.' The process may be gradual, but the backsliding condition is reached by forsaking God and taking up with something else.

In 2 Peter ii. 15 you will find a luminous word for workers—". . . forsaking the right way, they went astray, having followed the way of Balaam the son of Beor, who loved the hire of wrong-doing." Who was Balaam? A prophet. What was his way? Making a market of his gift. The New Testament speaks in three different ways about Balaam: "the way of Balaam," "the error of Balaam" (Jude 11) and "the teaching of Balaam" (Revelation ii. 14). The 'way' of Balaam is to make a market of one's gift, presuming on it, putting yourself in God's show-room. 'I am here as a specimen of what God can do.' Immediately a Christian begins to put himself into the 'show business,' that is the way towards backsliding. The 'error' of Balaam is seeing only the standard of natural morality and never discerning God's ways behind. Immediately a Christian gets into the way of following his own wise common-sense morality, rather than the dictates of the Spirit of God backing the Word of God, he is on the high road to backsliding. Beware how you guide your Christian life and your Christian experience. Are you simply taking the ordinary high standards of the world in your business? Beware, that is an error that leads to backsliding. 'Oh, well, they all do it, I must do the same.' That is the ordinary standard; if it conflicts in the tiniest degree with the clear standard of God, beware! It is an error that leads to the false doctrine which is the very heart

41

of backsliding, making a judicious mix-up between corrupt worldliness and godliness. That is the way blacksliding will begin, it is fixing your eyes on the wrong thing. The 'teaching' of Balaam is the corrupting of God's people. Balaam taught Balak to corrupt the people by enticing them to marry the women of Moab. That is the Old Testament incident, but what does it mean? It means trying to compromise between corrupt worldliness and Christian profession. These are three dangerous characteristics pointed out in the New Testament, and they are fruitful in backsliding.

When you come to deal with backsliders, one of the greatest dangers is that they spread their disease more quickly than any other. The presence of one backslider is a peril to a whole community. His or her influence is tenfold worse than a hundred sinners who have never been saved, and the worker for God who begins to deal with a backslider has to learn, first of all, his unutterable powerlessness to touch him.

Let us face the backslider now. Are you going to begin by asking him to receive the Spirit of God? You will have no answer. He may say, 'Yes, Lord, I am sorry, please give me the Holy Spirit,' but God won't. You won't find one case anywhere on record in the Old or New Testament in which

42

God deals with a backslider along those lines. Let me take as an illustration the parable in the fifteenth chapter of St. Luke. I know this parable is used in many ways, but I want to use it as a picture of the backslider. It is obvious why it is called 'The Parable of the Prodigal Son,' but it is not called so in the Bible, it is called 'The Parable of the Two Sons.' One son went away and spent his substance in riotous living, the other son stayed at home. Both are as bad as each other. The spirit of the stay-at-home was every bit as bad as the wild riot of the younger boy who went away.

Did the father send any message to the far country after the younger boy? There is no record of any message being sent. What did the younger boy have to do? He had to do exactly what is recorded in Hosea long before that picture was painted by our Lord—he had to return. Drawn by God? It does not say so. Read the fourteenth chapter of Hosea: "I will heal their backsliding"; but the backslider has to get up first, leave the pigs and what pigs eat, and go back to where he came from. Help granted him? None whatever. Messages from the home country? Not one. Tender touches of God's grace on his life? No. Can you picture that prodigal son returning, a degraded, sunken, sin-stained man, going back in all the cruel, bald daylight? Oh, it is a hard way to go back out of a backslider's hell; a hard, hard way! Every step of it is cruel, every moment is torture. But what happened? Before that younger son had got very far, the father saw him "and ran, and fell on his neck, and kissed him"!

Worker for God among backslidden souls, remember God's way, put the sting, if you can, into the backslider's soul that he may get up and come back to God, and what has he to do? Take with him words and say, 'By mine iniquity have I fallen.' Did the prodigal son take with him words? He did, he rehearsed them over and over again where he was amongst the pigs—'I will say to my father this and that,' he had it all by heart. Does Hosea say the same? He does: "Take with you words, and return unto the Lord, and say, 'By mine iniquity have I fallen.' " What does iniquity mean? Unequal dealing, turning out of the way.

Is there a backslider listening to this? Then rouse yourself and go back to God. 'But I feel no drawing.' You won't feel any. I do not find one instance in the Bible of God drawing a backslider in the same way that He draws a sinner. The word to the backslider is: *"Return."* "Take with you words, and return unto the Lord: say unto Him, Take away all iniquity."

Every Christian worker will bear me out in this next statement, that in dealing with a backslider, you are exhausted to the last drop of your energy. When we work with other classes, like those we have been touching on, God seems to supply grace at the very moment; but we need to remember that if in the other cases we need to rely on the Holy Ghost, we need to do so here a thousand-fold more.

Intercessory prayer for a backslider is a most instructive but a most trying work for God, and it will teach the worker that prayer is not only making petitions, but that prayer is breathing an atmosphere. The Christian Church nearly always separates those two; when it emphasizes the atmosphere of prayer, it forgets the petition; and when it emphasizes the petition it is apt to forget the atmosphere, but the two must go together, and you need to be freshly bathed moment by moment in the limpid life of God (if I may use the phrase) as you pray for your backslider. If ever the worker needs the wisdom that cometh from above, it is in the moment of dealing with a backslider. How am I going to awaken, how am I going to sting into action, a backslidden soul? How am I going to get that soul to go back?

I said just now that no message was sent to the

far country; God sends none, but, worker for God, will you be a message from the Father? Will you so bathe your life in the atmosphere of prayer that when you come in contact with a backslidden soul, it will awaken a remembrance of the Father, awaken a remembrance of what that soul once was? Will you let your life be like a bunch of flowers from the Father's home garden, just awakening for one moment a remembrance of what life once was, and then pass on, and pray and watch, and you will be mightily rewarded by God when you see that poor backslidden soul get up and go back to God, taking with him, words and saying, 'By mine iniquity have I fallen.'

If ever you hear a testimony along this line, 'I was a backslider, but, thank God, I am healed now,' do call a halt in that soul. Backsliding in the Bible is called by words used for the most shocking immorality. Can you imagine anybody who has been guilty of an awful moral crime talking about it in the glib, off-hand way some people talk about backsliding? When a backslider has been reclaimed by God and brought back, when he has returned and has been met by God, the memory of the past is too tremendously humiliating to be mentioned often, and when it is mentioned the atmosphere of the life is one of deep repentance towards God. Never sympathize with a backslider; do all in your power to goad him to return to God. If you cannot do it in words, do it by living in the atmosphere of God and awakening some remembrance of what he once was.

Another illustration of backsliding is in the twenty-third chapter of Matthew. It is not in reference to a person, but to the city of Jerusalem, but it gives a good picture of the way God deals with backsliders: "O Jerusalem, Jerusalem, which killeth the prophets, and stoneth them that are sent unto her! how often would I have gathered thy children together, even as a hen gathereth her chickens under her wings, and ye would not! Behold, your house is left unto you desolate. For I say unto you, Ye shall not see Me henceforth, till ye shall say, Blessed is He that cometh in the name of the Lord." "How often would I . . . and ye would not!"

Oh, if any here should be backsliders, let me counsel you to return to God, and tell Him that you have fallen away from Him by your own unequal doings. Take with you words and tell Him so, let the lash fall, and before you know another thing God will receive you! The prodigal son was all but choked on the bosom of his father before he got half his recital out; but he had to show that he was in earnest, he had to return first, and you must do the same.

Christian worker, if you have someone in your mind who is a backslider, one who did know the grace of God, who did run well but who has compromised, has a name to live but is dead, then God grant you may realize the filling up of "that which is behind the afflictions of Christ" in intercessory prayer. The backsliders are the most dangerous class under Heaven to touch, and no one but a man or woman who knows how to live bathed moment by moment in the love of God, who knows how to prevail in prayer, ought to touch the case of a backslider. It needs the wisdom that cometh from above, and if you have indeed been led by God to face such a life, do it on God's line. Do not try and bring God around by way of your ignorance; go along the clearly discerned lines that are given in His Word. Get that one to understand, either through his own intelligence or by praying, that he must return of his own accord.

"Take with you words, and return unto the Lord": . . . then God says, "I will heal their backsliding, I will love them freely."

Chapter V

THE WORKER AMONG THE 'TWO-FACED'

"Even so ye also outwardly appear righteous unto men, but within ye are full of hypocrisy and iniquity." Matthew xxiii. 28.

BY 'two-faced' I do not mean the kind of character John Bunyan refers to in his 'Mr. Facing-both-ways,' I mean a man guilty of internal hypocrisy. 'Two-faced' is simply a figure of speech for double dealing and falsehood. If you never have taken the trouble to go through the Bible to see how much God's Word has to say about the 'two-faced,' do it, and you will be surprised. Let me give you one or two passages to show you that this subject is not isolated or novel, not something taken because it sounds different from what is usually taken. It is taken because it describes a class of folk that are so difficult to deal with that we rarely hear them mentioned.

"Beware of false prophets, which come to you in sheep's clothing, but inwardly they are ravening wolves." (Matthew vii. 15.)

"For there shall arise false Christs, and false prophets, and shall show great signs and wonders; so as to lead astray, if possible, even the elect." (Matthew xxiv. 24, R.V.)

"Holding a form of godliness, but having denied the power thereof: from these also turn away. For of these are they that creep into houses, and take captive silly women laden with sins, led away by divers lusts." (2 Timothy iii. 5-6.)

These are simply a few of a number of passages in the Bible where the Spirit of God and our Lord draw the portrait of the 'two-faced.' Let me repeat it, the 'two-faced' are the hardest and most difficult people to work among. When we face the double-dealing, two-faced man of God, our hearts sink, our whole souls are terrified. We must not read the Bible like children. God requires us to read it as men and women, spiritual men and women, I mean. There are things in the Bible that stagger us, things that amaze and terrify; and the worker for God needs to understand not only the terrors of life around, but the terrors of life as God's Book reveals it.

Let us go back to the incident recorded in 2 Samuel xii. For subtlety, for amazing insight and sublime courage, Nathan is unequalled; and

what a soul was David to have in his list for God!
Would to God there were more preachers and
Christian workers after the stamp of Nathan.
David did not even begin to realize, after a year of
the grossest and most dastardly hypocrisy, that
Nathan was brandishing the sword straight into
his own conscience, and only when David had
made his answer and Nathan had heaved out the
strong denunciations of God and thrust the sword
straight home with, "Thou art the man!" did
David say, "I have sinned against the Lord."
There was no bungling about Nathan's work.

If you want to know how it was possible for a
mighty man of God like David to have sinned the
most wicked sin possible—I do not refer to adul-
tery or to murder, but to something infinitely
worse, a deep, subtle, inward hypocrisy, tremendous and profound; David lived it for a year and
administered justice while all the time he was a
'whited sepulchre'—you must first allow God to
examine deep down into the possibilities of your
own nature.

Mark how Nathan came to David. "And the
Lord sent Nathan unto David." Be sure, before
you face the hypocrite and the two-faced soul, that
God has sent you, and then use all the subtlety
you have from the knowledge of your own heart.

Any worker who has stood before God's all-search-ing eye for five minutes is not staggered at David's fall. Any heart-sin recorded is possible for any human heart, and why I say that the worker amongst the 'two-faced' will find it the hardest work is that he has to get his subtlety, his wisdom, not only from God on High, but from a strange, mighty probing of his own nature. If the worker for God is going to go all lengths for God for the cure of souls, he has to allow God to examine deep down the possibilities of his own nature. That is why it is hard to deal with the 'two-faced.' That is why, Christian worker, God will take you through disciplines and experiences that are not meant for your particular life; they are meant to make you ready for God to send as He sent Nathan. Then you can use that subtle sword. "Be ye therefore wise as serpents, and harmless as doves," said our Lord.

One solid year of deep heart-hypocrisy in King David's life, suddenly faced by Nathan, and watch how Nathan dealt with it. He used a parable of such God-given insight that David was blind as to his meaning. The sword went straight into David's conscience. As soon as David said, "The man that hath done this is a son of death," 'he is worthy of this and it shall be done,' instantly with sublime courage Nathan said, "Thou art the man." Then came the denunciations of God.

Worker for God, before you go among the infirm, the sick, the subtle, the hypocritical, let God deal with *you*. A child cannot wield the sword of the Spirit; it must be wielded by one fed on strong meat, one who has been deeply dealt with and examined by God's Spirit, in whom the last springs and possibilities of iniquity and wrong in his own nature have been disclosed to him that he may understand the marvel of God's grace.

Notice what the Apostle Paul did in a similar case. Read his Epistle to the Galatians, and see how he dealt with "false brethren"—"And that because of the false brethren privily brought in, who came in privily to spy out our liberty which we have in Christ Jesus, that they might bring us into bondage: to whom we gave place in the way of subjection, no, not for an hour; that the truth of the gospel might continue with you." (*ch*. ii, 4-5, R.V.) "False *brethren*"—mark the phrase, it is not mine, it is Paul's; they were brethren, though two-faced and untrue. What are we to do with them? "To whom we gave place in the way of subjection, no, not for an hour:"—why? That our views might be expounded? No. That they might be detected as hypocrites? No. "That the

53

truth of the gospel might continue with you."
"Let brotherly love continue." This is perfect love
to God; blazing, fiery zeal for God's honour, and
mercilessness against God's enemies. There is a
time to smite and a time to smile; a time to slay
and thrust straight home when the true, sterling
worth of your own repentance and the true, sterling worth of God's work of grace in your heart
are put to the test.

When these false brethren crept in unawares,
cunningly and craftily working against the honour
of the Lord Jesus Christ, how did Paul deal with
them? He withstood them; but be careful when
you deal with false brethren that you are on the
Apostle's line. If you dare to touch a false brother
and your life has not been riddled through by
God's searchlight, beware! If you are going to face
false brethren, if you are going to work for the
cure of the two-faced souls, if you are going to
work so that the thrust of the sword of the Spirit
will go straight home to the conscience, be pre-
pared first to be dealt with by God, or else, if you
begin to use your suspicions, your carping criti-
cisms instead of God's insight, you may get a reply
like this: "Jesus I know, and Paul I know; but who
are ye?" Set a thief to catch a thief, that is the
method of the world; but when God Almighty

sends a worker He sends one whom He has literally turned inside out, in a spiritual sense, one
whose disposition He has altered and allowed the
man or woman to know what He has done. There
is no false knowledge in that worker's life. That
worker goes straight for one purpose, the condem-
nation of the sinner, not to show his discernment,
but that he may bring the soul out of its duplicity,
out of its hypocrisy, into the light of God. Don't
begin to work from your carnal suspicions—how
many people mistake carnal suspicions for spiritual discernment! If God gives you a spirit of discernment, it is all right, there are times when He
does, but I would like to warn you—never ask God
to give you discernment. I have heard people ask
God to give them the spirit of discernment, and I
have felt constrained to say, 'Lord, lead that soul
not into temptation.'

If God is going to give you power, Christian
worker, to work for the cure of souls in their worst
form, among the 'two-faced' and the hypocritical,
remember, first He will give you such an insight
into the possibilities of your own sinfulness, and
then such a comprehension of the marvels of His
grace and wonderful salvation that you will have
all the subtlety Nathan had. You will not be silent, you will speak out. Oh, for more voices to

speak out when false doctrines are being taught! Would there were more to stand on the Nathan line, and wield the sword with all the wisdom of God's Spirit into the consciences of men, so that before men could know what they were driving at, the sword would have gone straight home with a 'Thou art the man!' Oh, for more of that kind of wisdom! To be right with God, so examined by God, that God can send the blade of the anecdote, or the blade of the parable, straight to the imagination, and while the imagination is busy the sword has gone straight home. Then comes the application without a moment's delay—"Thou art the man!" and the cry goes up, "I have sinned against the Lord." Then listen to Nathan's message to David afterwards: "And Nathan said unto David, The Lord also hath put away thy sin; thou shalt not die." What a message!

One more thing, in the multitude of all the talk and all the words nowadays, do not forget the first point—if you are going to work for the cure of souls, you cannot choose the kind of souls you are going to work with, and when God brings you face to face with a two-faced life, an inwardly hypocritical life, then you will understand what the examination of God's Spirit is in you. Then you will understand what it is to be used in God's hands as "a new sharp threshing instrument having teeth." Then you will know what it is for the sword of God to wound and bruise you until you can feel no more, that He may thrust home the sword that will kill the error and save the soul you are driving at. God grant we may understand that working for the cure of souls is not a babe's work; it is a man's work, requiring man's power, grasped and transformed by God Almighty, so that God can get straight through the worker to the man He is waiting for.

The one who stands beside Nathan in the New Testament is John the Baptist. There was no belittling of his message; when he was before Herod there was no trimming down the message to win his favour, no subtle telling a lie against himself for his own vanity. There is more of that done than most people think. Nathan and John the Baptist came straight from God, and if you come straight from God you have to be spotless; there must be nothing between you and God, Christian worker. John the Baptist came straight from God and talked straight for God. Do you talk straight for God? When the message you have to deliver, brother preacher, strikes straight home, don't water it down just a little. Go straight for God if you come from Him. Neither for fear nor favour alter the message. What happened to John the Baptist? He went straight back to God, minus his head. That was the result of his message.

The Spirit of God discerns more incapacity in workers in dealing with the 'two-faced' than in any other way. God grant we may so live under His searchlight that we may come straight from God and talk straight for God. It is easier to be silent than to obey God when you are face to face with a hypocrite, and if you are silent, you will get the applause of men. "When I say unto the wicked, Thou shalt surely die; and thou givest him not warning, nor speakest to warn the wicked from his way, to save his life; the same wicked man shall die in his iniquity; but his blood will I require at thine hand." (Ezekiel iii. 18.)

The next time you take a meeting, there may be a man after God's own heart there, but he has got on the line of internal hypocrisy and so may end as a son of perdition: you be faithful! You may have added to your list that day the soul of a David. But if you, seeing him and knowing him, begin to trim your message, God will require that man's blood at your hands. "If thou warn the wicked, and he turn not from his wickedness, nor from his wicked way, he shall die in his iniquity; but thou hast delivered thy soul." (Ezekiel iii. 19.)

Obey God at every price! But mark you, Christian worker, if you obey God, He is going to let you be tried to the point of agony. In dealing with souls, it is easy to dabble in shallow water with the abnormal, it is easy to dabble with the lost, it is easy to dabble with the ordinary, easily comprehended sinners, but when we begin to work with the backsliders and when we are face to face with the internal hypocrites, then we need the subtlety which comes through the Spirit of God, and many draw back. God grant many may go forward!

Chapter VI

THE WORKER AMONG SICK SOULS

"The destruction that wasteth at noonday."
Psalm xci. 6.

I WONDER if this has been growing clear to you, that we cannot understand the cases we have to deal with. One of the first things a worker for God has to learn by experience is that strangely obvious lesson, that none of us can understand the cases we meet to work with. Then how can we work for the cure of them? Remember the first principles we laid down: By knowing Jesus Christ for ourselves experimentally, and then by relying on the Holy Spirit.

"And I hated all my labour wherein I laboured under the sun." (Ecclesiastes ii. 18, R.V.) These words were written by Solomon, the wisest man that ever lived, and you will find the last summing up of all he says is the statement of a sick soul, not a healthy-minded soul, not a vigorous sunshiny hopeful soul, but exactly the opposite.

We have spoken about the worker for the cure

of souls among the 'hardy annuals,' the hardy sinners, nothing sick about them, they are healthy and happy and wholesome. Now I want to take exactly the opposite kind of people. If our religion is only a religion of cheerfulness for the healthy-minded, it is no good for London, because more than half the people there, a great deal more than half, are not able to be cheerful, their minds and consciences and bodies are so twisted and tortured that exactly the opposite seems to be their portion. All the talking and preaching about healthy-mindedness, about cheering up and living in the sunshine will never touch that crowd. If all Jesus Christ can do is to tell a man he has to cheer up when he is miserable; if all the worker for God can do is to tell a man he has no business to have the 'blues'—I say if that is all Jesus Christ's religion can do, then it is a failure. But the wonder of our Lord Jesus Christ is just this, that you can face Him with any kind of men or women you like, and He can cure them and put them into a right relationship with God.

The New Testament mentions quite a few of these sick souls. We will take two just now— Thomas and Mary Magdalene. Thomas was naturally gloomy, not happy and healthy-minded, that was not the way he was made. He was loyal

61

to Jesus Christ, but he took the 'sick' view of life; he always thought the worst was going to happen. You remember that when Lazarus died and Jesus said He was going to Bethany, Thomas said, "Let us also go that we may die with Him." It was no use going to Thomas and preaching the gospel of cheerfulness; you cannot alter facts by saying 'Cheer up.' What did Jesus Christ do for Thomas? He brought him into personal contact with Himself and altered him entirely. (See John xx. 24-29.)

Mary Magdalene was another type of the sick soul, tortured and afflicted. It was no use going to Mary and telling her to believe there was no such thing as the devil, no such thing as sin, she was absolutely incapable of taking the first step. What did Jesus Christ do for Mary Magdalene? Help her to be happy when she was miserable? Help her to realize that there was no such thing as demon-possession? No. He turned out the demons and healed her. (Luke viii. 2.)

In the second chapter of Hebrews we read of a great crowd of sick souls who were subject to bondage through fear of death, and Jesus Christ came to deliver them from their bondage; and in 1 Corinthians xi. 30 (R.V.) we read, "For this cause many among you are weak and sickly, and not a few sleep." I have simply run over these cases to show that there is sufficient indication in the Book of God for us to recognize that there are sick souls naturally.

One word about the physical condition of people. There is a threshold to our nerves, that is, a place where the nerves begin to record. Some people's nerves do not record things as quickly as others. Some people have what is called the 'misery' threshold of nerves, the threshold where the nerves begin to record is much lower down than it is in other people. Take it in connection with sound, some people can sleep in a tremendous racket, noise makes not the slightest difference to them. The ear gathers up vibrations, and only when those vibrations are quick enough do we hear. If the threshold of our hearing were lower, we should hear anything that makes waves in the atmosphere, we should hear the flowers grow; everything that grows makes a motion in the atmosphere. The majority of us have a threshold that is high up, and we cannot hear unless there is sufficient vibration in the atmosphere. Get a nervous system where the threshold of nerves is low, and life is an abject torture to that one wherever he goes. What is the good of telling him to cheer up? There is a bigger problem there than we can touch. That one is in contact with forces which the majority of us know nothing about; he is tortured by things we never hear, tortured by things we never feel. Such people take a very gloomy view of life; they cannot help it.

When a worker meets a soul like that, what is he going to do—preach the gospel of temperament, 'Cheer up and look on the bright side,' or preach Jesus Christ? 'The gospel of cheerfulness' is a catchword of the day—it may be all very well among people who are naturally cheerful, but what about the folk who cannot be cheerful, who through no fault of their own have bodies where the threshold of their nerves is so low down that life is a misery? Read the second chapter of Hebrews again, and you will find it says that Jesus Christ took on Him not the nature of angels, but —"since then the children are sharers in flesh and blood, He also Himself in like manner partook of the same" (R.V.). Jesus Christ took on Him a flesh and blood nature with nerves and He knows exactly how the human frame is tuned and how it is tortured. Every Christian worker ought to know how to bring the sick souls, the souls that take the gloomy view, to Jesus Christ. These people will accept all you say about the need to receive His Spirit, but nothing happens; they do not cheer up. How are we going to bring Jesus Christ into contact with them?

If you read Acts x. 38 (R.V.) you will find Peter says a wonderful thing about Jesus of Nazareth— "how that God anointed Him with the Holy Ghost and with power; who went about doing good, and healing all that were oppressed of the devil." Peter had just awakened to the fact that "God is no respecter of persons," and it is important to notice that he says God anointed *Jesus of Nazareth* with the Holy Ghost and with power. Peter had never preached like that before. When he preached to the Jews he had presented Jesus Christ as being first the Son of God. As soon as he came in contact with the outside crowd who were not Jews, who were not religious, the Spirit of God makes him present Him as Jesus of Nazareth. When men are being led of the Spirit of God, they never preach their convictions.

But I want you to notice what it was Peter said Jesus of Nazareth did; He healed "all that were oppressed of the devil." There are only two religions that accept gloom as a fact (I mean by gloom, sin, anguish and misery, the things that make people feel that life is not worth living), viz., Buddhism and Christianity. Every other religion ignores it. This is the age of the gospel of cheerful-

65

ness. We are told to ignore sin, ignore the gloomy people, and yet more than half the human race is gloomy. Sum up your own circle of acquaintances, and then draw your inference. Go over the list, and before long you will have come across one who is gloomy, he has a 'sick' view of things, and you cannot alter that one. How are you going to get that oppression taken off? Tell him to take so many weeks' holiday by the sea? Take iron pills and tonics? No! Living in the peace and joy of God's forgiveness and favour is the only thing that will brighten up and bring cheerfulness to such an one. Only when God takes a life in hand can there come deliverance from the 'blues,' deliverance from fits of depression, discouragement and all such moods. The Scriptures are full of admonitions to rejoice, to praise God, to sing aloud for joy; but only when one has a cause to rejoice, to praise, and to sing aloud, can these things truly be done from the heart. In the physical realm the average sick man does not take a very bright view of life, and with the sick in soul true brightness and cheer are an impossibility. Until the soul is cured there is always an underlying dread and fear which steals away the gladness and the "joy unspeakable and full of glory" which God wishes to be the portion of all His children.

66

In dealing with sick souls, we must remember the Master's way, how He went to the root of the matter. Hear Him as He said, time and again when one was brought to Him for physical healing, "Thy sins be forgiven thee." Dig out the "root of bitterness," then there can be no fruit to sour the life and set the nerves on edge.

My brother or sister, if you are a worker for Jesus Christ, He will open your eyes wide to the fact that sin and misery and anguish are not imaginary, they are real. Anguish is as real as joy; tired, jangled and tortured nerves are as real as nerves in order. Low threshold nerves, where everything is an exquisite misery, are as real as high threshold nerves where nothing is misery. Listen to this, they are Luther's own words:

" 'I am utterly weary of life. I pray the Lord will come forthwith and carry me hence. Let Him come above all with His last judgment. I will stretch out my neck, the thunder will burst forth and I shall be at rest.' And having a necklace of white agates in his hand at the time, he added: 'O God, grant that it may come without delay. I would readily eat up this necklace to-day for the judgment to come to-morrow.' The Electress Dowager one day, when Luther was dining with her, said to him, 'Doctor, I wish you may live forty years to come.' 'Madame,' replied he, 'rather than live forty years more, I would give up my chance of Paradise.' "

That was Luther speaking at the end of his life. What produced the misery? He saw the havoc the Reformation had wrought, he did not see the good, he was too near it.

There was the same thing in Goethe's writings; in 1824 he writes:

"I will say nothing against the course of my existence, but at the bottom it has been nothing but pain and burden, and I can affirm that, during the whole of my seventy-five years, I have not had four weeks of genuine well-being. It has been the perpetual rolling of a rock that must be raised up again."

Robert Louis Stevenson said that three hours out of every five he was insane with misery. John Stuart Mill said that life was not worth living after you were a boy.

This is not fiction, these are human facts. What does Christian Science do—ignores them! New Thought—ignores them! Mind Cure—ignores them! Jesus Christ opens our eyes to these facts, but here comes the difficulty: how am I to get Jesus Christ in contact with these sick souls?

In the first place, will you realize that you do not know how to do it? I want to lay that one principle down very strongly. If you think you know how to present Jesus Christ to a soul, you will never be able to do it. But if you will learn how to rely on the Holy Ghost, believing that Jesus Christ can do it, then I make bold to state that He will do it. If you get your little compartment of texts, and search them out and say, 'I know how to deal with this soul,' you will never be able to deal with it; but if you realize your absolute helplessness and say, 'My God, I cannot touch this life, I do not know where to begin, but I believe that Thou canst do it,' then you can do something.

It is wonderful to see Jesus Christ slip His coolness and His balm through tired and jangled nerves, turn out demons, alter the whole outlook and lift the life into a totally new relationship. Have you ever seen Him do that? I have seen Him do it twice in my lifetime, and I will never forget it. While you watch and while you realize the marvellous work of God going on in those gloomy, tortured lives, it is as if you were bathed in the sunlight of the Presence of God in a way you never are until you are face to face with one of these cases that make you realize your own utter helplessness and the power of Jesus Christ.

It was Jesus Christ coming in contact with Thomas that altered his gloom; the disciples' testimony could not do it. 'Thomas, we have seen the Lord,' and out of the agony of his sick soul,

Thomas says, 'I cannot, I dare not, believe!' "Except I shall see in His hands the print of the nails, and put my finger into the print of the nails, and put my hand into His side, I will not believe." The testimony of the disciples was not the slightest bit of use, but when Jesus Christ came in contact with him, all was different. "Then saith He to Thomas, Reach hither thy finger, and see My hands; and reach hither thy hand, and put it into My side; and be not faithless, but believing. Thomas answered and said unto Him, My Lord and my God."

And Mary Magdalene—what did Jesus Christ do for her? He turned the demons out of her. "Mary that was called Magdalene, from whom seven devils had gone out." (Luke viii. 2, R.V.) Demon possession means that one body can hold several personalities. Do you believe that? Very few people do nowadays, but it is an awful fact, not only in the New Testament, but outside the New Testament, that one body may be the holder of more than one personality. How much room does thought take up? None. Personality partakes of the nature of thought. How much room does personality take up? None. "And when He was come forth upon the land, there met Him a certain man out of the city, who had demons; . . .

and Jesus asked him, What is thy name? And he said, Legion; for many demons were entered into him." (Luke viii. 27-30, R.V.) Many devils in one man—the modern man laughs at the idea, but the poor, tortured, demon-possessed man is left alone. Jesus Christ heals him and delivers him of them all.

God grant us the grace so to rely on the Holy Ghost, so to know our ignorance, so to get out of the way with our knowledge, that we will let the Holy Ghost bring the Majestic Christ face to face with the diseased, sick folk we meet. The majority of workers are in the road with their convictions of how God is going to work, there is no real, living, stirring, vital reliance on the Holy Ghost which places straight before the tortured, stricken soul the Mighty Lord Jesus. God grant we may so rely on the Holy Spirit that we may allow Him to introduce through the agony of our intercession— that is the point, through the agony of vicarious intercession—the Living, Mighty Christ! My brother and sister, are you willing to allow Jesus Christ to use every bit of your life to trample on in His way to another soul? Do you know anything about spending one costly drop of blood in vicarious intercession? There is nothing worked in the way of result in answer to prayer that does not cost somebody something. "Who in the days of His flesh, having offered up prayers and supplications with strong crying and tears. . . ." When you meet your sick soul, do you cry awhile and then go home and sleep, instead of taking that soul before God and vicariously interceding until by reliance on the Holy Spirit, Jesus Christ is presented to that darkened, difficult life? Blessed be the Name of God, there is no case too hard for Jesus Christ!

One more thing—what is it produces sick souls? Our emotions are associated with certain things and the value of those things to us lies in the emotion they start. For instance, you have some things in your home that are of no use to anybody on earth, but to you they are enormously valuable. Let something come in and destroy your emotions and associations, and what kind of a world are you in? A world in which suicide is the only outlet. Let some paralysis come and destroy your emotions, all your associated ideas with things, with people, with houses, with friends, with work, and the light is gone out of the sky, the power and the joy out of life, everything is paralyzed, and the universe is one black prison-house. What will produce that? Look at the prodigal son. Have you ever dropped the plumb-line down into his heart

72

and tried to fathom one phase only of his cry—"I have sinned against heaven, and in thy sight"? Oh, the agony of the soul that has been paralyzed on the inside—the gloom, the darkness, and the shadow! No preaching of the gospel of good cheer will touch that; it is only the great Life-giving, Life-imparting Christ Who can touch it. Oh, my brother or sister, you have lately been brought face to face with some case and you have said, 'This is conviction of sin,' but you know it is not. You have tried all the Scriptural teaching you know, with no result. You have tried to advocate this thing and that, but no result, and you have been humiliated to the dust before God. Is not this the reason—you have been trying to find out what is wrong? God will never show you what is wrong; that is not your business. What He wants us to do is to bring the case to Him: 'Lord, use my inter-cession as a channel through which Thou canst reach that soul.' God grant that we may be so cen-tred in Him that He can use us in that wonderful way.

Chapter VII

THE WORKER AMONG THE STUPID
SOULS

"Behold, I have played the fool, and have erred exceedingly." 1 *Samuel* xxvi. 21.

THIS is a statement made by the prophet of the Most High God, and a King of Israel. Before I read some passages from God's Book to show you that the stupid soul is continually brought before the attention of the reader of God's Word, I would like you to notice what the word 'stupid' means. It does not mean ignorant, but anything formed or done without reason or judgment. Ignorance is being without knowledge "and the times of this ignorance God winked at" (Acts xvii. 30), i.e., "overlooked" (R.V.). Do distinguish between ignorance and stupidity!

Let us look at one or two passages:

"And Moses and Aaron gathered the assembly together before the rock, and he said unto them, Hear now, ye rebels; shall we bring you forth water out of this rock?" (Numbers xx. 10, R.V.)

"Because they provoked his spirit, so that he spake unadvisedly with his lips." (Psalm cvi. 33.)

"When anyone heareth the word of the kingdom, and understandeth it not, then cometh the evil one, and snatcheth away that which hath been sown in his heart." (Matthew xiii. 19, R.V.)

"For we ourselves also were sometimes foolish." (Titus iii. 3.)

"For of these are they that creep into houses, and take captive silly women laden with sins, led away by divers lusts, ever learning, and never able to come to the knowledge of the truth." (2 Timothy iii. 6-7, R.V.)

"For when by reason of the time ye ought to be teachers, ye have need again that someone teach you the rudiments of the first principles of the oracles of God; and are become such as have need of milk, and not of solid food." (Hebrews v. 12, R.V.)

My reason for running over these passages is that the truth may sink into our minds that the Bible lays a tremendous emphasis on the fact that there are stupid souls.

Now let us get back to Saul. I know it is not the usual way of summing up Saul, but I want to take him as an illustration of the stupid soul. Read the description of Saul in 1 Samuel ix. 2 (R.V.)—

"And he had a son, whose name was Saul, a choice young man and a goodly: and there was not among the children of Israel a goodlier person than he: from his shoulders and upward he was higher than any of the people." His physique was magnificent, his bodily presence wonderful, but he was amazingly stupid. Samuel was known everywhere, he was such a mighty prophet and man of God, but there were two people who did not know him—a man called Kish and his son Saul; they spent their time breeding asses, and knew nothing whatever about Samuel. Saul actually met Samuel and asked him if he could tell him where the seer was! How did Saul get the first inkling of who Samuel was? Through one of his father's servants. If you are a stupid soul spiritually, do get in touch with a godly servant—in touch with someone who does know the seer! And Samuel said to him, "I am the seer; . . . and in the morning I will let thee go, and will tell thee all that is in thine heart." Then we read that "God gave him another heart." If Saul had gone on in obedience to God's Word, his life would have fulfilled God's intention; but instead of that, he is a model for all time of a stupid soul.

What are we to do when we come across stupid souls? Ignorant souls we can deal with, they need knowledge; the stupid soul does not need knowledge; the stupid soul needs to have the word of God until it is worried by it. The difficulty is how the worker is to get the word of God into its right place. Jesus Christ says the stupid soul is the one that hears the word and does not understand it. "When anyone heareth the word of the kingdom, and understandeth it not, . . ." (Matthew xiii. 19.) Does God hold a man culpable for being stupid spiritually? He certainly does. Every case of stupidity recorded in the Bible is punished by God. How can I get the word of God into a stupid soul? Read 1 Samuel xv., and see how Samuel dealt with Saul. 'The commandment of God, why did you not obey that?' Take the Apostle Paul, the very same thing: "O foolish Galatians, who hath bewitched you, that ye should not obey the truth . . . ?" And our Lord's own words: "O foolish men, and slow of heart to believe after all that the prophets have spoken!"

This is the time, Christian worker, when you must use the word until you get it wedged in somehow in that stupid soul, until it rankles and worries its way to the soul's salvation or destruction, and there was never a class that will drive a worker closer to God than the stupid soul, they will tax every bit of patience and endurance you have. They always pretend to want to do something—"ever learning, and never able to come to the knowledge of the truth"—why? They would not obey the word they heard, that is the beginning. You remember Samuel asked Saul if he had fulfilled the word of God with regard to the Amalekites, and Saul said he had: "Blessed be thou of the Lord: I have performed the commandment of the Lord. And Samuel said, What meaneth then this bleating of the sheep in mine ears, and the lowing of the oxen which I hear?" Pretending, that is the first characteristic of the stupid soul. Again in his last agony, when Saul went off on the spiritualistic line, Samuel says the same thing: "Because thou obeyedst not the voice of the Lord."

You will come across the stupid soul in connection with the elementary work of grace, the new birth: 'I want to be sanctified, I have done this and that and the other.' Well, be perfectly certain they have not; if those things had been done, there would be no "bleating of the sheep," no provision for the lusts of the flesh, none of the laying down of careful lines for the development of things that ought not to be in the Christian life. Is any soul beginning to deceive itself? That is the danger of stupidity; when once it begins to disobey God's

Word ever so little, it begins to deceive itself. 'Well, God is very hard with me, I did fulfil the word of God, I did what I knew how to.' How is the worker going to get the word of God driven straight home? As you wait before God, there is no class for which God will give you passages of Scripture more quickly than for this class, and at your peril you lower the standard of the word of God.

The first thing I want to note with regard to the worker is this, never sympathize with a stupid soul. Sympathize with the sick soul; sympathize with the abnormal soul—sympathy is needed for nearly every soul but the stupid soul, but never sympathize with stupidity in the approach of a soul to God. Watch Samuel, watch Paul and watch our Lord—the word of God, the word of God, the word of God, first, second and last; no sympathy, no help, only the word of God.

Have you ever noticed that if a stupid soul hears a word of God too often it may turn again and trample on that word? A man who ultimately became a great power for God, on his own testimony, said that the centre of his life was once full of this kind of stupidity. He was a so-called worker for God for several years, until he came across this verse: "Ye are not your own: for ye were bought with a price," and he said wherever he went that verse kept chiding him; when he read a book he would come across it; when he heard a sermon it would be from that text, until he said, 'At last I took my penknife and cut the verse out of every Bible I had.' Then the Spirit of God awakened him as to what he had done, and he confessed the whole thing before God and God forgave him his stupidity.

Christian worker, when God gives you a word for a soul who is stupid, keep at it. This is the time when you have to keep using the verse God gives you for a soul: every time you meet him, every time you write to him, every time you talk to him. The only way you will stir up that one out of his stupidity is by driving home the word of God, and presently you will see that stupid soul saved from perdition, if it has not gone as far away from God as Saul, and as far away as many a stupid soul will go for lack of faithful workers. But if you as a worker have one strand of stupidity in you, one characteristic in your life where you are apt to make statements and judgments unreasonably, beware that your message does not become a boomerang. A boomerang is a peculiar weapon so balanced that when you fling it as far from you as you can, it comes back and hits you!

God's Word is always a boomerang to the worker
who uses it if he is not right with Him.

Worker for God, are you quite sure there is no
strand of stupidity in you? Are you quite sure you
are not in the category of those who are ever learning, but never coming to the knowledge of the
truth? Are you facing something about which you
are very willing to be stupid? Then the word of
God in your hand will come straight back to you
when you try to deal with another soul—"Thou
art the man." But if you are living rightly yourself, then keep on the line of pressing the word
home. Will you just run over in your mind,
worker, the stupid souls you have in your Sunday-
school class, in your Church services—are you gloss-
ing over the word God gave you for them? Hammer at it morning, noon and night; if you cannot
get at their ears, get at them by prayer. If it is
Luke xi. 13, then keep at it until they say, 'I wish
you would be quiet about Luke xi. 13; is there
nothing else in the Bible but that verse?' But what
about "the bleating of the sheep"? That is what
keeps you to your point, and God will never let
you get away from it. If a man says he has received
the Spirit of God and yet has not gone on with
God, there is always a word of God to tell him
why, and if you are a worker for God you will be

a persistent annoyance and aggravation to that one whenever you meet him, until ultimately he comes to the place where he will praise God for the annoyance. Every worker can give instances of God awakening the stupid soul by persistence on the one point. This is the stern element in Christian work.

How did Jesus Christ deal with the foolishness or the stupidity of the two disciples on the road to Emmaus? These disciples were good, simple souls, honest and true, but they had become stupid, blinded by their own grief, their own point of view. What did Jesus say to them? "O fools, and slow of heart to believe all that the prophets have spoken." The word 'fool' is often used in the New Testament, but not always in the same way, here it means literally, 'My little imbecile children, when will you believe all that the prophets have spoken?' This is stupidity of a totally different order, a stupidity that Jesus deals with very pointedly, but very patiently. It is a stupidity that has obliterated the interpretation of the word of God because of personal grief and perplexity. Is Jesus Christ coming to you by the Spirit and saying, 'My little imbecile child, when will you believe what I say?' Is there any particular thing in your life, Christian worker, that you have become

82

THE WORKER AMONG THE STUPID SOULS

slow of heart to believe? Do not let the stupidity grow. Get the word of God for it. Oh, if there ever was a need, it is for people to search and ransack this Book and get at what God says. How much time have you given to finding out what the Bible has to say? An hour a day? 'Oh, I cannot give an hour.' Half an hour? 'Oh no, I cannot give that.' Five minutes? 'Yes, I could do that.' Well, have you done it? Five minutes a day out of twenty-four hours to find out what the word of God says! No wonder God says, "My people doth not consider."

Never water down the word of God to the understanding of your people. Would that God the Holy Ghost would thunder that through you as He has thundered it through me! Never drag down the word of God to anybody's understanding. Hammer at it, keep at it, and drive at it, till the laziness is taken out of people's hearts and brains and bodies, and they are willing to face what this Book has to say about their condition, and face it with the sterling earnestness they use to see what the newspapers have to say when they are on the hunt for a new situation. God grant we may learn the imperativeness of getting at what the word of God has to say about our particular need, then perhaps we will begin to understand why we have that need.

"The words that I speak unto you, they are spirit, and they are life." The word of God is "a lamp" and "a light," but when people get off on the 'stupid' lines, it is all instincts, impressions, vague ideas—"ever learning, and never able to come to the knowledge of the truth." Then is the time when men of reprobate mind creep in and lead astray. There are a number of 'creepers' stealing in nowadays, religious 'creepers,' and they will steal into your soul, my brother and sister, just where you are stupid. Has something been said to you recently from the word of God that has awakened you with a startling realization to the fact that you have not obeyed God on a certain point? Then may God bring you face to face with a faithful worker who will bring the same thing to you, whatever it is, until you get through. When the word of God has begun its piercing even to the dividing of soul and spirit, it will have its wonder-working way and heal and re-create and dissipate the stupidity.

Chapter VIII

THE WORKER AND THE PASSION FOR SOULS

"To the weak I became weak, that I might gain the weak: I am become all things to all men, that I may by all means save some." 1 *Corinthians* ix. 22 (R.V.).

YOU hear people say that Paul showed his wonderful breadth of mind, his culture and generosity, his gentleness and patience, by becoming all things to all men. He did nothing of the sort; he said, "I am become all things to all men" for one purpose only—"that I may by all means save some." He did not say, 'I became all things to all men that I might show what a wonderful being I am.' There is no thought of himself in the whole matter.

The phrase 'a passion for souls' is a dangerous one; a passion for souls may be either a diseased lust or a Divine life. Let me give you a specimen of it as a diseased lust—"Woe unto you, scribes and Pharisees, hypocrites! for ye compass sea and

land to make one proselyte; and when he is become so, ye make him twofold more a son of hell
than yourselves." (Matthew xxiii. 15, R.V.) 'Proselyte' is a technical word for convert, and our Lord
is showing that these Pharisees had a great passion
for souls which He stamped as of the devil; and
if you read the thirteenth chapter of Acts you will
find a remarkable thing occurs—the proselytes became exactly what Jesus Christ said they would,
"twofold more a son of hell," far more supersti-
tious and fanatical; the devout women alluded to
who persecuted the apostles were proselytes (*vv.*
43-50). In Revelation xiii. 11-17, you will find
again the passion for souls as a diseased lust. I
refer to the beast coming up out of the earth; the
consummation of his power was to get the souls
of men into one solid mass.

But have we got clearly in our minds what the
passion for souls as a Divine life is? Read James
v. 19-20 (R.V.): "My brethren, if any among you
do err from the truth, and one convert him; let
him know, that he which converteth a sinner from
the error of his way shall save a soul from death,
and shall cover a multitude of sins." The Apostle
is talking to those whom we understand as Chris-
tians, 'If any among vou, my brethren, do err from
the truth . . .'

Again, our Lord in speaking to His disciples, used some striking phrases, all of which refer to this passion for souls, in Matthew iv. 18-22, He speaks about making them "fishers of men"; in John xxi. 15-17, He says, "Feed My sheep," a striking phrase which has a direct bearing on the right passion for souls: and after the Resurrection He said, "Go ye therefore, and make disciples of all the nations." (Matthew xxviii. 16-20, R.V.) I want to take these three phrases as a guide for the worker in regard to this great passion for souls.

There is a telling pathos about the twenty-first chapter of John; all the disciples had forsaken the Shepherd, and Jesus says, 'Now never you forsake the flock, you become broken bread and poured-out wine and feed the flock.' God grant we may understand that the passion for souls is not a placid, scientifically worked-out thing, it compresses all the energy of heart and brain and body in one consuming drive, day and night from the beginning of life to the end—a consuming, fiery, living passion. That was the characteristic of our Lord's life, and of the lives of all the disciples after Pentecost, and of the life of the Apostle Paul.

Take first of all the phrase "fishers of men." There are one or two significant things about that figure of speech. The early disciples were fishermen, and the Spirit of God seems to point out that their earthly employment was a parable of their Divine vocation. David was a shepherd, he became the shepherd of Israel. Paul was a tent-maker; he was used by God for making men's bodies into tabernacles of the Holy Ghost. I wonder how many of you know what it is to be out all night at sea fishing? I do. Before the early dawn, about three or four in the morning, you feel so amazingly cold and so amazingly indifferent that you don't know whether you care for anything, and there is an exact counterpart of those nights in work for God. Do you know what it is to have a relationship to God so consuming, a personal, passionate devotion to Jesus Christ so powerful that it will stand you in good stead through every cold night, while you are watching and waiting to land men for God? It is those cold nights of waiting, cold nights of praying and of preaching, when, like Gideon's army over again, many leave and forsake and just the few are left, that are the test.

What a marvellous illustration fishing is, especially fishing with the net, and Jesus Christ told the disciples He would make them "fishers of men," catchers of men. Unless we have this divine passion for souls burning in us because of our personal love for Jesus Christ, we will quit the work before we are much older. It is an easy business to be a fisherman when you have all the enthusiasm of the catch, everybody then wants to be a fisherman. Just as everybody comes in with the shout and the 'Hallelujah' when revival signs are abroad; but God is wanting those who through long nights, through difficult days of spiritual toil, have been trying to let down their nets to catch the fish. Oh, the skill, the patience, the gentleness and the endurance that are needed for this passion for souls; a sense that men are perishing don't do it; only one thing will do it, a blazing, passionate devotion to the Lord Jesus Christ, an all-consuming passion. Then there is no night so long, no work so hard and no crowd so difficult, but that love will outlast it all.

God grant that we may see that our passion for souls springs from that on which the Moravian Mission founded its enterprise—the fifty-third chapter of Isaiah; behind every heathen face, behind every face besotted with sin, they saw the Face of the Son of God; behind every broken piece of earthenware, they saw Jesus Christ; behind every down-trodden mass of human corruption, they saw Calvary. That was the passion that was their motive. God grant we may get it back again. That is the deep, true, evangelical note for the passion for souls, the consuming passion that transfigures a man's self, that transfigures a woman's self, and makes him or her indeed wise and patient and able fishers of men.

Beware of the people who tell you how to fish! I know a good many people who have tried to learn how to fish from books, but they never did learn. The only way to learn how to fish is to fish! An old sea-captain whom I know very well, who has been a fisherman all his days, told me he met a man who had published a book on how to catch fish. The captain took him out in his boat; they stayed out four hours, but he didn't have enough strength to put one piece of line over the boat, he was too seasick. That was the instructor of how to catch fish!

Beware of the books that tell you how to catch men. Go to Calvary, and let God Almighty deal with you until you understand the meaning of the tremendous cost to our Lord Jesus Christ, and then go out to catch men. God grant we may get away from the instructors on how to catch fish and get out into the fishing business!

Mrs. Howard Hooker pointed out in an address one day that the disciples when Jesus Christ called them were mending their nets, and she made the remark, "The majority of Christian people are always washing and mending their nets; but when Jesus Christ comes along, He tells them to launch out and let them down; it is the only way to catch fish." God grant we may see the aptness of Jesus Christ's words, "I will make you fishers of men." Is there some Sunday-school teacher to whom it has been a cold, cold year in your class, have you gone home every Sunday afternoon with a heart like lead, and have you cried to God, saying, 'O God, I have prayed and asked and longed, but not one of these lives can I get for Thee'? God grant, if you feel like that, you may go back to Calvary again and again, until the Holy Ghost expounds to you the tremendous, passionate love of the Lord Jesus Christ.

Have you ever noticed one thing about the early disciples, viz., that in every case the choice is the Lord's, not the man's. "Ye have not chosen Me, but I have chosen you." Jesus turned away everyone who came to Him and said, 'I want to be Your disciple.' Jesus Christ knows the men and women He wants. God grant that His choice may fall on every one of us, and that we may learn with patience and discipline how He is going to teach us to be patient, to be powerful and to be passionate in His service! Never losing heart, never being discouraged, never being excited over a big catch.

Many a worker has rendered himself useless to God by his undue hilarity over a big revival for God. "Notwithstanding in this rejoice not, that the spirits are subject to you," said Jesus; "but rather rejoice, because your names are written in heaven." God grant we may understand that the mainspring of our passion for souls must be a personal, passionate devotion to the Lord Jesus Christ.

Then the shepherding of the flock. Read John xxi., every one of the disciples had forsaken Jesus; the night had got too cold, too dark, their own grief was too overwhelming, and they all forsook Him and fled. Then Jesus came to them in the upper room and imparted to them His Spirit, and now He gives them this commission—"Feed My lambs"; "Tend My sheep"; "Feed My sheep."

Now both the fisherman's art and the shepherd's art sound poetical until you have tried them! I begin to thank God that in my boyhood and early manhood I had to take so many tries at a good many things. I did not like it at the time, but I am thankful now I had to do shepherding in the highlands of Scotland. When you have to carry across your shoulders a dirty old wether and bring it down the mountain-side, you will soon know whether shepherding is poetry or not; you will soon know whether it is not the most taxing, the most exhausting and the most exasperating work; and Jesus uses the illustration for the passion for souls. Quiet, judicious knowing how to do it won't do it; passion alone will do it. One of the grandest men I ever knew was a sheep-farmer, and he told me of his nephew whom he was trying to train as a sheep-farmer (he is now a minister in Canada)—'The boy cannot learn sheep-farming; it must be born in him.' That used to be the old shepherd's great theory, that you could not teach a man how to look after sheep unless it was born in him. Jesus Christ drives home the very same truth to the disciples. To whom did He say, "Feed My lambs"? To Peter. Who was Peter? A very wayward sheep. Peter had not only forsaken Jesus Christ, he denied with oaths and curses he ever knew Him, and now that Peter has received the Holy Spirit and is personally, passionately devoted to Jesus Christ, do you think that anybody could have such patience with young converts as Peter? Who was it that wrote, "Tend the flock of God which is among you, exercising the oversight, not of constraint, but willingly, according unto God"? Peter. Peter had marvellously learned through his own experience how to be patient, how to be tender, how to be full of grateful watchfulness

93

over all the Lord's sheep.

But there is another aspect. When Jesus said, "Feed My sheep," He gave Peter nothing to feed them with. This is a tremendous point. You cannot nourish the flock of God unless you are rightly related to the Shepherd. You may be the mouthpiece for God's truth to the unsaved, but you cannot nourish the flock of God which is among you unless you are rightly related to the Shepherd, unless you are willing to let God use you as broken bread and poured-out wine to feed His sheep. Much-tried Christian worker, you are not understanding what God is putting you through; perhaps this is what He is fitting you for, to teach you how to feed His sheep, to tend the flock of God. Sunday-school teacher, perhaps Jesus Christ is teaching you how He is going to make you broken bread and poured-out wine. Take some time, Christian worker, over your Bible, and see what God has to say about shepherds, about hireling shepherds. This work of feeding and tending sheep is hard work, arduous work, and love for the sheep alone will not do it, you must have a consuming love for the great Shepherd, the Lord Jesus Christ; that is the point I want to leave impressed. Love for men as men will never stand the strain. In order to catch men for the Lord Jesus

94

Christ, you must love Jesus Christ absolutely, beyond all others. You must have a consuming passion of love, then He will flow through you in a passion of love and yearning and draw men to Himself.

Then, lastly, "make disciples of all the nations." (Matthew xxviii. 16-20.) "Making yourselves ensamples to the flock," says Peter. What does that mean? Be a walking, talking, living example of what you preach, in every silent moment of your life, known and unknown; bear the scrutiny of God, until you prove that you are indeed an example of what He can do, and then "make disciples of all the nations." Now we come to the great, grand idea of the universal and spiritual aspect of the work of a Christian. There is no respect of persons with God, no respect of nations with God —here, there, anywhere and everywhere, wherever God likes to stir up your nest and fling you, disciple all the nations. When souls are born again into the kingdom of God the Church of Christ makes a tremendous rejoicing, as it ought to make, but then what does it do? When God brings souls to you who have been brought into His kingdom by His sovereign work of grace, what have you to do? Disciple them, and the only way you can disciple them is not by making them proselytes of your views, but by teaching them to do what Jesus commanded you to do and you have done. Watch the Apostle Paul's testimony—"who shall bring you into remembrance of *my ways which be in Christ*." How often the Apostle Paul says, when talking to his converts, "Ye are our glory and joy." Sunday-school teacher, can you say, 'God has manifested His grace in me, and if you come to the same place He will manifest it in you'? Or, do you have to say, 'Do as I say, but not as I do'? Before we can disciple all the nations, we ourselves must be where we want other people to be. Watch again that matchless Apostle's life, the consuming, passionate agony of his soul was for the converts, not for the crowd outside; discipling is the one stamp of that mature Apostle's life. "My little children, of whom I am again in travail until Christ be formed in you." (Galatians iv. 19, R.V.)

Another thing: Sunday-school worker, and Christian worker, and minister, you must be farther on and higher up than those you are leading, and you must be going on all the time. Now we come to the meaning of God's discipling of various workers, of His removing some workers and of putting others over the heads of others. Beware of being stationary! God grant that we may be going on with Him continually so that we can disciple all we come in contact with. When a young convert asks you a question—'Can God deliver me from the disposition of sin?' what will you say? If you cannot answer, 'Thank God, He can deliver you,' then beware! God may have to remove your candlestick as a teacher, as a worker. How does the Apostle Paul finish that wonderful chapter, 1 Corinthians ix.—"I buffet my body, and bring it into bondage: lest by any means, after that I have preached to others, I myself should be rejected," cast away as reprobate silver. God grant that no Christian worker may fall from the heaven of his usefulness because he refuses to go on with God!

If you have cooled down in your spiritual life, Christian worker, has it not come about that some weeks ago, or some months ago, you were asked a question and you could not answer it, and you ought to have been able to answer it? It was a practical, pointed question about what God could do for a man's soul, or for his body, and you could not answer it, why? Because the side issue of your own life was not clear; and until you make that issue clear, you are left as reprobate silver. You have preached to others? Yes, and God blessed your preaching, but from the second you begin to neglect the side issues of your life, that moment God begins to leave you alone as a worker for

97

Him. God grant you may get back again, all the avenues clearly open to Him, avenues of heart and head and body and soul, back premises and front premises, underground and overhead, and all around, clear and open to God! Then let the questions come from anywhere, questions that touch the head, questions that touch the back record, questions that touch the underneath record— 'Can God restore the years the cankerworm hath eaten?' 'Can God alter the build of a man's mind?' 'Can God destroy laziness out of a man?' I was talking to an elderly minister the other day, and speaking of ministers and Christian workers generally, he said, "The great defect in all branches of Christian work is laziness." The only cure for laziness is to be filled with the life of God to such an overwhelming extent that He can spend you to the last cell of your body, to the last drop of your blood, for His own glory. God grant that the consuming passion for souls for Jesus Christ's sake may get hold of us as never before!

One other thing I want you to notice with regard to this passion for souls. God will put you through many mills that are never meant for you, mills you never would be put through but that He wants to make you good bread for His little ones to eat. Christian worker, you see the meaning now of that hard place you have been in; God wants to make you bread well enough baked until you are His 'standard' bread, and then He can break you for the feeble amongst the flock. What is the consuming passion in the Apostle Paul's life? Devotion to the Lord Jesus Christ. "For I could wish that I myself were anathema from Christ for my brethren's sake, my kinsmen according to the flesh." "And I will most gladly spend and be spent out for your souls." Christian worker, have you lost out in that consuming passion? If you are getting cooled down, visit the Cross of the Lord Jesus Christ and ask the Spirit of God to give you insight into its meaning, ask Him that you may understand it in a new way. Then go forth, and—

"Measure thy life by loss instead of gain;
 Not by the wine drunk, but the wine poured forth."

Chapter IX

THE GOD-APPROVED WORKER

"Give diligence to present thyself approved unto God, a workman that needeth not to be ashamed, handling aright the word of truth." 2 *Timothy* ii. 15.

WE have been dealing with the worker for the cure of souls, now I want to deal with the prevention which is better than cure. How can a man or woman become a workman approved unto God? Read 1 Timothy iv. 16—"Take heed to thyself, and to thy teaching." If you forget everything else, do not forget that verse. The word "heed" occurs again in Acts iii. 5 and xx. 28. It means to concentrate, to screw your mind down, fix it, limit it, curb it, confine it, rivet it on yourself and on your teaching. It is a strong word, a powerful word, a word that grips, a rousing word. That is what we have to do if we are going to be workmen approved unto God.

But I want you to notice first of all who is talking and who he is talking to. It is the Apostle Paul talking to Timothy, or writing to Timothy, or sending a message to Timothy. Paul's method was that of apprenticeship, that is always God's method of training workers. In the old days when artists used to have apprentices, they used to put the boy in charge of mixing paints and in between doing this he would watch the artist paint, and slowly, bit by bit, doing the hard work and watching the master work, he would learn to 'take heed.' That was Paul's method. Timothy had a good mother and a godly grandmother, and he was trained spiritually in this apprentice style. If you are going to be a worker for the cure of souls, God will bring you under masters and teachers. That is the method God always uses. He does not use anyone who is undisciplined. Thank God for every worker who was ever placed under apprenticeship!

"Take heed to thyself." That is not self-realization; it is self-preparation, and the first thing I want to notice about self-preparation is in chapter iv. 13, "Give attendance to reading." The word "reading" does not mean what we understand by reading—opening a book and looking at it; it means what we understand in Scotland by expository preaching. 'Listen to that kind of discourse, Timothy, read that kind of manuscript, and when you open your mouth, follow that specimen.'

What is expository preaching? It is not taking a text out of its setting and using it as a title; it means that the verse is taken in its setting and applied where it is meant to apply. I wonder how many workers are taking heed to their reading in this expository way. I wonder what kind of preacher you delight to listen to? What kind of book you like to read, what kind of instruction you delight to listen to? Paul tells Timothy to take heed, first of all, to this important thing. "Give attendance to reading."

In order to get this more crystallized in our minds, read Nehemiah viii. 4-5: "And Ezra the scribe stood upon a pulpit of wood, which they had made for the purpose; . . . And Ezra opened the book in the sight of all the people; (for he was above all the people;) and when he opened it, all the people stood up." That is the God-ordained method of expounding God's Word, and it is as if Paul said to Timothy, 'When you read, when you listen and when you teach, remember God's time-honoured method—get upon your pulpit of wood as an official.' There are two kinds of official worker—the one who may become a castaway; that is what the Apostle Paul dreaded—"I keep under my body, and bring it into subjection: lest that by any means, when I have preached to others, I my-

self should be a castaway." The other kind of
worker is the one who is an example of what he
teaches. But the point to notice here is that the
person who expounds God's Word has to be seen
of all the people; if his sermons are written, let
the people see they are written; if he is reading
from the Bible, let the people see that he is; if he
is reading someone else's sermon, let him say so.
These are not trifling things, they are tremendously important things, and the word 'reading'
covers them all. 'Search after that kind of preacher,
Timothy, and listen to him.'

Worker for God—and I speak this to myself as
well as to you—what do you fasten your mind on
when you listen to a preacher, when you read a
book? When Jesus Christ said, "Thou shalt love
the Lord thy God with all thy heart," He did not
stop there, He went on to say, "and with all thy
soul, and with all thy *mind*, and with all thy
strength." Oh, I wish I had time, I would kindle
you by telling you of some folks I know who have
lifted themselves out of the very gutter of ig-
nominy and ignorance by sheer grind in the secular callings of life. Would to God we had the same
stick-to-it energy in God's line! Many a lad have
I known in Scotland who has worked hard day and
night to attain a scholarship in secular callings,

and are we to be behind them? This word of the Apostle Paul's is used in that connection—"take heed," concentrate, stick at it, fix the mind on it. Give heed to reading, be careful of your self-preparation. God grant that we may be approved unto God by what we build in. When Paul mentions the matter of conversation, he says, 'See that your speech is edifying'—good building-up stuff, not sanctimonious talk, but real solid stuff that makes people stronger in the Word of God, stronger in character, stronger in practical life.

Paul says to Timothy another thing, "Of these things put them in remembrance, charging them in the sight of the Lord, that they strive not about words, to no profit, to the subverting of them that hear." And again, "Shun profane babblings: for they will proceed further in ungodliness, and their word will eat as doth a gangrene." And again, "But foolish and ignorant questionings refuse, knowing that they gender strifes." 'Don't argue! don't enter into controversy at any price.' Paul told Timothy not to enter into controversy at any price, and Paul was the arch-controversialist himself! Paul spent most of his days in controversy, and yet he tells Timothy not to argue! But have you read Paul's method of controversy? Paul put himself with amazing courtesy and amazing insight and amazing tenderness into the place of the man he was disputing with. The reason Paul tells Timothy not to argue, and the reason he tells me not to argue, and the reason he tells you not to argue, is that we argue from our own point of view. We argue not for the truth's sake, we argue to prove we are right. God grant that we may learn to take heed lest we get switched off on arguing. Is there some worker for God likely to be twisted and turned aside by battling for the faith? Let me read you some words I have jotted down in my Bible:

"Oh, the unmitigated curse of controversy! Oh, the detestable passions that corrections and contradictions kindle up to fury in the proud heart of man! Eschew controversy, my brethren, as you would eschew the entrance to hell itself. Let them have it their way; let them talk; let them write; let them correct you; let them traduce you; let them judge and condemn you; let them slay you. Rather let the truth of God suffer itself, than that love suffer. You have not enough of the divine nature in you to be a controversialist." (Dr. Alexander Whyte.) "Heal me," prays St. Augustine, again and again, "of this lust of mine of always vindicating myself."

Take heed, fix your mind, never be wheedled

into controversy. Let the Spirit of God contro-
vert. One of my greatest snares ever since I became a Christian is this very thing. I know what
it means, I know the galling humiliation and
agony in days that have gone by of wanting to
argue the point out, and I know, possibly better
than any of you, the inwardness of the point that
the Apostle Paul is driving at with Timothy—
'Don't do it, Timothy; stop, you will damage your
own soul, you will hinder the truth of God, you
will bruise the souls you talk to.' God grant we
may fix and concentrate our minds and take heed
to this! Take heed to yourself, take heed how you
read, and above all don't argue. Have you learned
this, Christian worker, that when any soul begins
to discuss the baptism with the Holy Spirit, it is
time you got out of the way? they have a controversy with the Holy Ghost, not with you. 'Sanctification' is not a man's term; it is God's: 'the baptism with the Holy Ghost' is not man's conception,
it is God's, and when a soul begins to argue on
these matters, remember, worker for God, it is
the Holy Spirit they are arguing with, the Word
of God they are haggling about. God grant we
may not hinder those who are battling their way
slowly into the light.

One more thing: Paul tells Timothy to "preach

the word; be instant in season, out of season."
(2 Timothy iv. 2.) Watch the setting of that. Timothy was fragile in body physically, Paul is frequently telling him how to take care of his body,
and yet here is the Apostle telling this young man
who is feeble in body to preach the word in season and out of season, what does he mean? To take
every opportunity of preaching the word? He does
not mean any such thing; he means 'preach the
word in season or out of season with regard to
yourself, never let your bodily condition hinder
your preaching.' The Apostle Paul is driving at
laziness, heart-sloth. God grant we may learn how
to be instant in season and out of season, always
at it, night and day, whether we feel like it or not.
When you come to read deeper down between the
lines in the Bible, you will find running all
through it the awful curse on laziness and spiritual sloth. Has it come on you mentally, Christian
worker? Then may God rouse you up to get to
reading, to get to work with your pencil and note-
book, in cars and out of cars, behind the counter,
anywhere. God grant we may be roused up in
the spiritual domain to put energy and vim into
our work and never say, 'I can't'; 'I have no time.'
Of course you have not, no man worthy of the
name ought to have time to give to God, he has

to take it from other things until he knows how God values time. Take heed to yourself, and never allow anything to produce laziness and sloth.

And lastly, "Continue in these things; for in doing this thou shalt save both thyself and them that hear thee." (1 Timothy iv. 16.) There is the charter for the worker, he is to be a pattern. "Let no man despise thy youth" (v. 12). Was Paul telling Timothy to stand up and say, 'I know I am only a youngster, but I defy any man to contradict me'? Paul is saying, 'Do not let youth be despised in you,' and then he tells him to be "an ensample to them that believe, in word, in manner of life, in love, in faith and in purity." The only way youth can save itself from being despised is by the life being in keeping with the profession, the teaching backed by it, the conversation, the manner of life, the purity, the clean, vigorous, upright manhood; not only a worker sent from God, but an ensample of what God can do. The baptism with the Holy Ghost and fire made the disciples the incarnation of what they taught. God grant that we may be the pattern of what we preach, that we may be workmen approved unto God, rightly dividing the word of truth.

Chapter X

THE HOLY WORKER

"But of the rest durst no man join himself to them: . . . and believers were the more added to the Lord, . . ." Acts v. 13-14.

I WANT to end where I began, with the character of the worker. God grant we may understand the power of a holy worker for God. I don't mean a holiness worker; what we need is *holy* workers—there is a big difference.

"But of the rest durst no man join himself to them: . . . and believers were the more added to the Lord." Have you caught the contrast?—a holy dread and a holy discipleship, they always go together. The souls who stand true to God are those whom God's Spirit has added.

"And great fear came upon"—the crowd outside? No, "upon the whole church, and upon all that heard these things." And then a wonderful thing happened—a great benediction fell on the multitude outside, "and believers were the more added to the Lord, multitudes both of men and women."

I want to deal with this holy dread and holy discipleship. "Knowing therefore the terror of the Lord, we persuade men." It is necessary for those of us who are workers for God to allow the Spirit of God to lift the veil sometimes and strike terror through us. We take our salvation and our sanctification too cheaply, without realizing that Jesus Christ went through the deep waters of uttermost damnation that we might have it. We read that a great fear came across the members of the early Church: "And great fear came upon the whole church, and upon all that heard these things,"—why? They realized, what we have to realize, that the Pentecostal dispensation produces not only Pentecostal living people, but liars to the Holy Ghost. Look for one moment at Ananias. "But Peter said, Ananias, why hath Satan filled thy heart to lie to the Holy Ghost, and to keep back part of the price of the land? . . . How is it that thou hast conceived this thing in thy heart?" Read the last verses of chapter iv, "Barnabas . . . having a field, sold it, and brought the money, and laid it at the apostles' feet." It is probable that indirectly Barnabas was responsible for Ananias. Barnabas had done a wonderful thing and doubtless he was praised for it, and Ananias wanted to equal it. We need to live steadfastly in the presence of God so that when we are praised we don't arouse the spirit of envy, the spirit that makes a man want to do something, not because he loves God, but because he wants to emulate us. Let me ask you who are workers, and let me ask myself, 'Why do you work for the salvation of souls? Why do you want to spend and be spent for others?' 'Mrs. So-and-so does it and she is my ideal.' Beware! 'I watched Mr. So-and-so and I want to be like him.' Beware! God grant we may see that the great need of every worker is a first-hand acquaintance with Jesus Christ which puts to death the spirit of ambition. Ambition has murder at its heart; our Lord showed His disciples that ambition is impossible in His kingdom, 'Except ye become as little children, ye shall in no wise enter into the kingdom of heaven.' Our attitude is to be one of steadfast personal devotion to Jesus Christ, not 'measuring ourselves by ourselves, and comparing ourselves with ourselves.' Among the last words Mr. Reader Harris wrote was this phrase —"Don't imitate." That means far more than mere external imitation, it means in the deep spiritual sense what I am trying to bring before you now—don't try and do something for God because somebody else is doing it. Oh, the amount of instigation in God's work that comes along that line!

Mark one more thing. Peter said to Ananias, "Thou hast not lied unto men, but unto God." Christian worker, how much time are you giving to prayer, to reading your Bible? 'Oh, I am giving all the time I can.' Be careful that you are not lying to the Holy Ghost. Pentecostal lying begins in this way, dragging down the intense holiness of God which keeps a man right with God in every detail of his life. Let us examine ourselves the next time we say, 'I have not time,' or, 'I give all the time I can to the study of God's Word,' 'I give all the time I can to praying.' God grant we may be put on the alert on these lines that we may not be found lying to the Holy Ghost. May these words come with warning and with scrutiny and bring our souls face to face with God.

And now holy discipleship. "But of the rest durst no man join himself to them." I wonder, Christian worker, if we realize what we are doing when we ask a man to give himself to Jesus Christ, do we know what we are telling him to do? We are telling him to kill for ever his right to himself, we are telling him that he has to be holy, chaste to the last recess of his bodily life. If ever that word needed thundering in Christian work it needs thundering to-day, chastity in bodily life.

You cannot have holiness without a chaste physical life. Oh, the sapping of the power of God because of unchaste men and women who preach His Gospel. God grant that the touch of God may startle and amaze any self-indulgent man or woman. May we remember the next time we go forth to speak for God that our bodies are the temples of the Holy Ghost. Immediately we realize this and bind ourselves to those who realize the same truth, God will begin to do His marvels in saving men unto Himself. So many of us are being caught up by the benedictions that fall on the crowd outside. The crowd outside will magnify the power of God, but none of those who are not right with God dare join them. If any Christian worker wants to get the strong grip of iron into his soul and into his work for God, let him read the Acts of the Apostles. The power of those holy workers checked impostors on the right hand and on the left. A Holy Ghost movement always brings impostors, parasites, by the legion. The only safeguard for the Christian worker is, 'Holiness unto the Lord.' If we are living rightly with God, living holy lives in secret and in public, God puts a wall of fire round about us. Beware of calling anything holiness that is only winsome and sweet to the world.

God grant we may never lose the touch of God that produces the holy dread.

Now we come to our last point. This holy discipleship will result in multitudes being added to the Lord. "And believers were the more added to the Lord, multitudes both of men and women." Is not that what we want, multitudes added to the Lord? How is it to be done? By captivating addresses? Mrs. Howard Hooker reminded us the other night when speaking of her father, that his preaching was always on the line of sanctification; a great many people could not stand it and consequently went away. It has always been the same and always will be. When once the holiness of God is manifested in human lives and in preaching (and the two go together), these two things happen: a great number durst not join themselves, and multitudes are added to the Lord. Never think that the blessing and benediction of God on the outside crowd is all. It is a mere fringe. Men and women are blessed, their bodies are healed, devils are turned out; but the point is that multitudes of those who believe are added to the Lord.

God grant that we may stand steadfastly true to Him and live this holy life. As we go forth tonight, let us remember Jesus Christ's commission,

114

"All power is given unto Me in heaven and in earth. Go ye therefore and make disciples of all the nations." As we examine our hearts before God, let us renew our covenant with Him.

7079